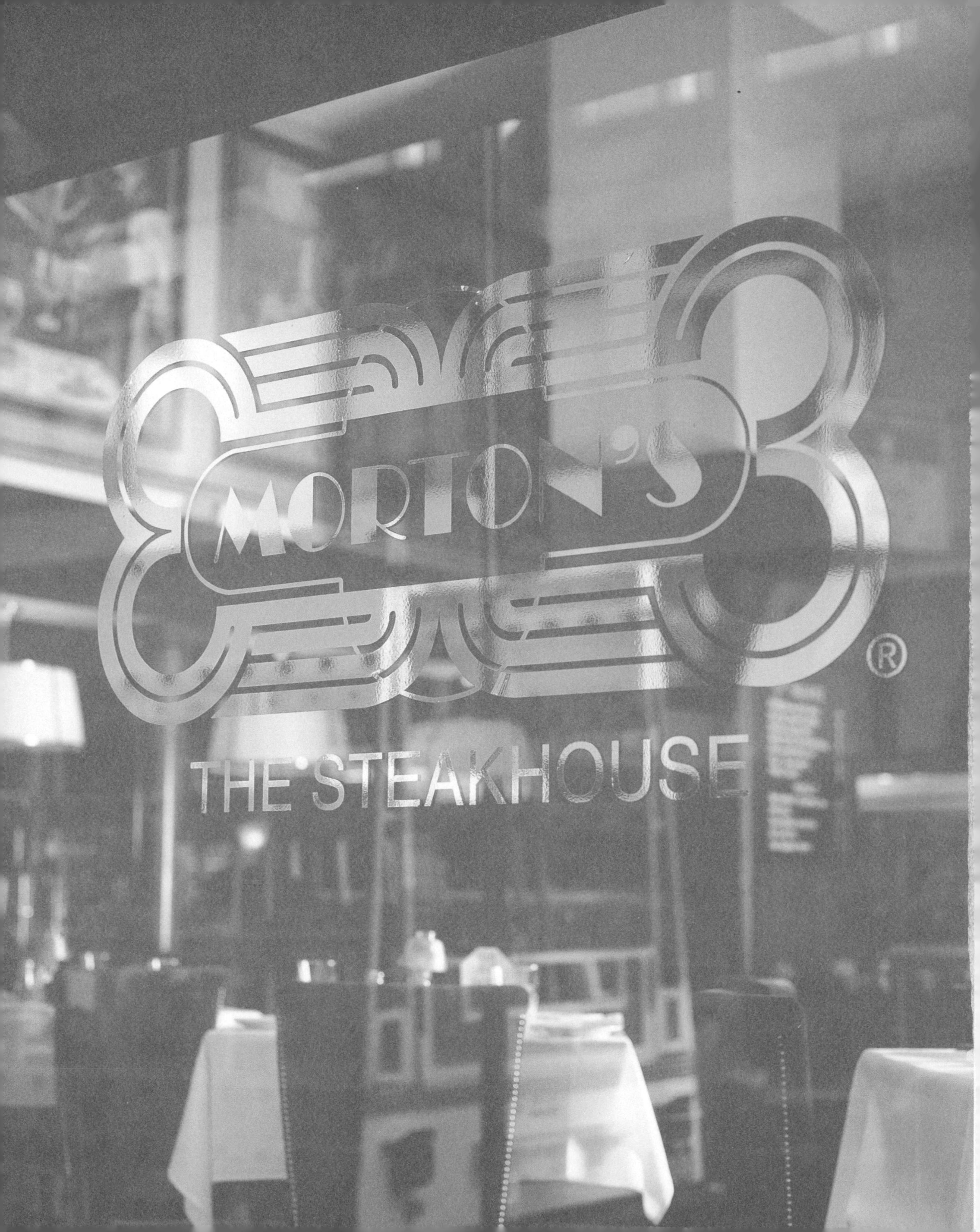
MORTON'S
®
THE STEAKHOUSE

MORTON'S
STEAK BIBLE

KLAUS FRITSCH WITH MARY GOODBODY

MORTON'S STEAK BIBLE

RECIPES & LORE FROM THE LEGENDARY STEAKHOUSE

Clarkson Potter/Publishers
New York

Published in the United States by Clarkson Potter/Publishers,
an imprint of the Crown Publishing Group, a division of Random House, Inc., New York.
www.crownpublishing.com
www.clarksonpotter.com

Clarkson N. Potter is a trademark and Potter and colophon are registered trademarks of Random House, Inc.

Library of Congress Cataloging-in-Publication Data
Fritsch, Klaus.
Morton's steak bible : recipes and lore from the legendary steakhouse / by Klaus Fritsch with Mary Goodbody.
Includes index.
1. Cookery (Beef)   2. Morton's, The Steakhouse (Firm)   I. Goodbody, Mary.   II. Title.
TX749.5.B43F75   2005
641.6'62—dc22   2005016622

ISBN-13: 978-1-4000-9794-4
ISBN-10: 1-4000-9794-0

Printed in the United States of America

Design by 3+Co.

10 9 8 7 6 5 4 3 2

First Edition

BAR
12·21
AT MORTON'S

Bar Bites Available from 5:00 p.m. to Closing

BAR BITES

OYSTERS ON THE HALF SHELL	14
COLOSSAL SHRIMP COCKTAIL	19
CHICKEN GOUJONETTES	8
THREE PRIME CHEESEBURGERS	10
CRAB AND ARTICHOKE DIP	11
FILET SANDWICHES	10
POTATO SKINS	7

MORTINIS

THE MORTONS COSMOPOLITAN	12
APPLETINI	11
PALM BEACH INFUSION	11
KEY LIME PIE	11
THE GEORGIA PEACH	11

CONTENTS

INTRODUCTION

At Morton's we love steak. This should come as no surprise. We are known for serving the best prime steaks available and cooking them to perfection. But our love of good food extends far beyond beef, although we always find our way back to big, juicy steaks.

We understand how much you love a great steak. And we hope if you're reading this book you will never again ruin a thick, expensive steak, whether you are cooking it on a grill or under a broiler. With our help, your days of tough, overcooked meat should be over. But there's more to our book than steak. With these recipes, you can re-create the Morton's Steakhouse experience even as you plan a full, rounded meal that's sure to please your family or guests, regardless of how discriminating their palates.

We wrote this book to share our expertise, our food, and our story with everyone who loves to cook and appreciates good American food. It's for home cooks and food lovers who may never eat at a Morton's Steakhouse but who know that we, better than anyone else, can direct them when they fire up the grill. It's also for our guests, who often ask when we'll have a cookbook.

Here it is!

A FEW WORDS ABOUT MORTON'S

When guests walk into Morton's Steakhouse, they know what they will get—no surprises, no fad-driven innovation, just perfectly cooked steaks or chops, well-poured drinks, fresh salads and side dishes, and luscious desserts. Recipes for all these, including the cocktails, are on the following pages, modified for home cooks and home kitchens.

Our restaurants are so consistently managed that whether you visit us in Hong Kong, Denver, or Boston, you can expect excellence. Morton's is the most recognized fine-dining brand in the world, and because of this, we take quality control very seriously. Legions of loyal guests appreciate this.

All Morton's Steakhouses share similar decor and atmosphere. The interiors retain the timeless feel of an old-fashioned Midwestern steakhouse, with mahogany panels, spacious leather booths, etched glass partitions displaying the distinctive Morton's logo, and classic snow-white tablecloths. Subdued lighting, warm brickwork, and walls adorned with celebrity photographs and a large collection of LeRoy Neiman serigraphs and prints add to the intimacy. You may feel you are dining in a restaurant with a long history, but in fact the first Morton's Steakhouse opened its doors in 1978 in Chicago. Since then, we have opened seventy restaurants in the United States, Canada, and Asia.

The Morton's menu is consistent at all of its restaurants, offering generous portions of perfectly aged beef, including a 24-ounce porterhouse, a 20-ounce New York strip, and a 14-ounce double-cut filet mignon. We also serve other cuts of beef, as well as lamb, chicken, and seafood. While our restaurant portions are known to be generous, for this book we cut them back to be more realistic for the home cook.

We understand our mission clearly. We pay close attention to quality, service, and consistency. We don't add items to our menu without tremendous thought and testing in the kitchen. This commitment to excellence was in place when we opened for business in 1978 and continues to this day. In 1989 Allen J. Bernstein bought Morton's and formed Morton's Restaurant Group; the company has been growing ever since.

Ours is a simple vision and one that has served us well over the years. On the other hand, had we listened to every critic and taken everyone's "surefire advice" along the way, Morton's would not be what it has become today. As Arnie Morton said when he and I founded the restaurant, Morton's is a neighborhood saloon for the rich and for people who like to splurge now and then. It still is.

1

HOW TO COOK
LIKE A STEAKHOUSE

My job is to oversee our restaurants. I travel throughout the year, visiting the chefs and staff at our worldwide locations. Whenever a new restaurant opens, I am there. Usually our corporate chef, Chris Rook, is a few steps ahead of me, since his job is to get the new kitchen up and running so that it meets Morton's culinary and efficiency expectations.

All the kitchens in our seventy restaurants are similar. They share an open design that looks out on the dining room so that guests can watch our chefs at work and see the fires under our grills. This proximity also helps us deliver food directly to the table the moment it's ready. When a steak comes off the grill, glistening with its natural juices, we want it to get to our guest immediately. This requires careful timing in the kitchen so every dish for a table is ready at once. It also calls for attentiveness and cooperation in the dining room; our entire staff knows that if a plate is ready, whoever is closest to the kitchen carries it to the table—the maître d', the manager, or a server.

This attention to detail and service was part of our initial vision. In the old days, we were one of only a few fine-dining steakhouses. But now competitors open with regularity, or as I have sometimes said, like mushrooms after a spring rain. This is good for us—competition is always healthy—because examining what others do only reinforces our vision. And we like what we see!

STEAK: WHAT WE DO BEST

Since day one, we have used the same suppliers for our aged prime beef and other meat. Long before Arnie Morton and I joined forces to found the steakhouse, I bought meat from the same two Chicago companies we rely on today. These guys know what we want. They select the best of their inventory for us—and if it doesn't meet our standards, we send it back.

In the old days, Jimmy the Butcher cut all the steaks for the restaurant in the back room. By the time we opened two or three more restaurants, we took Jimmy's specifications to the suppliers, who hand-cut the meat for us. Nowadays, all Morton's steaks, chops, and roasts are precut and packed in Cryovac for delivery and storage. The meat is never frozen.

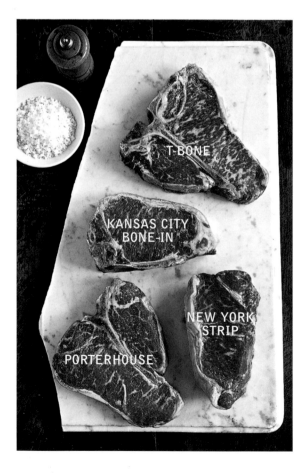

It arrives in our kitchens fresh, cut, trimmed, and ready to cook.

We remove the meat from our coolers 30 to 60 minutes before cooking. I can't emphasize to the home cook how important this is. The meat will cook far more evenly and the cooking times in our recipes will be most accurate if you allow meat to reach room temperature before cooking it. The larger the piece of meat, the more crucial this is. (If the day is very hot and humid, stay close to the 30-minute mark.)

When you buy steak for cooking at home, you most likely will not be able to get the same quality we serve at Morton's. We serve aged prime beef, which means it's the best there is. A meat's grade is determined by the marbling, the weblike structure of fat running through the muscle. The finer, more even, and more generous the marbling, the higher the grade of the beef.

Most beef available to consumers is USDA choice, although there are times when you can get USDA prime. If you see it, try it. High-end choice beef is nearly as good, so don't be disappointed if you can't get prime. Less than 2 percent of the nation's beef supply earns the designation prime, and most of that ends up at steakhouses such as ours. When you ask the butcher to cut steaks for you, whether you are buying prime or choice, ask for center cuts. These tend to be the most tender and are less apt to have any tough veins.

My number one recommendation is to buy beef and other meat from a butcher you know. He will cut steaks and chops to your specifications, and he can steer you in the direction of what is best in his meat case. If you don't have a butcher nearby, I suggest you order beef from a reputable catalog or online service. This tends to be expensive, but there are some very good

PRIME RIB ROAST

RIBEYE

BONE-IN RIBEYE

Web sites that sell premium products; when you plan a special meal, you won't be disappointed. If you end up at the supermarket, ask the butcher to cut the meat for you rather than buying it from the packaged meat case.

When you buy beef, examine it for marbling. Beef should be a true red with creamy flecks of fat. Ribeye steaks often have a natural thick kernel (or deposit) of fat. Avoid beef that is bright red, browning, or two-toned; has yellowish fat; or is either undermarbled or overly fatty. Beef should be capped with a thick coat of ivory fat.

If you buy chopped meat, buy it from a butcher who grinds it for you. Some butchers may not grind the meat in front of you, but they will assure you that they grind their own. If you buy it already packaged from a supermarket, it should be a nice, even red mixed with creamy pieces of fat. We like ground sirloin with a ratio of lean meat to fat of 80:20. Try for a similar balance.

COOKING THE STEAK

As it cooks, steak loses moisture, and so it naturally shrinks. That 2-inch-thick strip steak you started with may measure only 1½ inches after it's cooked. I suggest you err on the side of under- rather than overcooking. You can always toss the meat back on the grill if it's undercooked.

We cook our steaks over a very hot fire. You may choose to cook them over hot coals or gas elements in a gas grill, or under a broiler. The temperature should be hot enough to sear the meat the instant it hits the grill rack. For most of our steak recipes, we instruct you to let the coals reach medium-hot. Gas grills, which are a little cooler, should be turned up to high. Broilers, by definition, are very hot.

If your charcoal or gas grill has a thermometer, the grill is considered **hot** when the thermometer registers between 425° and 450°F. If you hold your open palm about 4 inches over the heat, you won't be able to keep it there for longer than 2 seconds, and the charcoal will be lightly covered with ash and glow red. For **medium-hot** temperatures, the thermometer will register between 375° and 425°F. You won't be able to hold your palm over the heat for longer than 3 seconds, and the coals will have a slightly thicker coating of gray ash covering the deep red glow. For **medium** heat, the thermometer will register between 325° and 375°F. You will be able to hold your palm over the heat for 4 seconds, and the gray ash will significantly cover the red, glowing coals.

Let the meat come to room temperature before you grill it. This can take from 30 minutes to an hour. On a very hot summer day, or if your kitchen is particularly warm, this won't take too long. You never want to leave raw meat at room temperature for longer than an hour.

We flavor our meat with seasoned salt and nothing more. At the steakhouses, we use our own blend of salt and spices, which we buy from a supplier who makes it to our specifications. This is not easy to duplicate in the home kitchen, so for the recipes here we suggest you use your favorite brand. Lawry's Seasoned Salt is readily available.

Once we've seasoned the meat, we cook it over a very hot fire and serve it right off the grill. You probably won't be able to duplicate this same heat intensity at home, so we tested all the recipes in a home kitchen using ordinary broilers, gas grills, and charcoal grills. We were impressed with the results.

When you grill, the outside of the steak chars. A nice, crispy, lightly charred crust is the goal. If the meat's surface turns black and seems too charred, move the meat to a cooler part of the grill.

TIMING THE STEAK

We test steaks' doneness by time and by their feel. Both are subjective. Timing will vary from broiler to broiler and grill to grill, and we hope you view the cooking times in our recipes as guides, not absolutes.

Not all cuts of meat feel exactly the same, but as they cook, all reach different degrees of doneness in similar ways. If you press lightly on a raw strip steak or T-bone, it will feel firmer than a raw filet mignon. As these cuts cook, they will feel different as they reach each stage of doneness, but the principles will be the same.

To understand our method, follow these guidelines:

Hold your hand out, palm up. Poke the pad at the base of the thumb. This is how rare meat feels when it's ready to come off the grill or out from under the broiler. (The strip steak may feel a little different from the filet mignon, but not remarkably; if you feel them both when they are raw, you'll be able to determine this.) The area of your hand between the thumb pad and the center of the palm feels how medium-rare meat feels; the middle of the palm is how medium meat feels; and the base of the pinkie is how well-done meat feels.

There are other tests for doneness. For example, if you like medium-rare meat, a bone-in steak is done when the meat is still firmly attached to the bone. When the meat on a porterhouse or T-bone starts to pull away from the bone, it is past medium-rare and on its way to medium.

Watch the juices that naturally escape from the meat. The steak won't release much juice when the meat in the middle is still red, but when it starts to turn pink inside, it will. If you notice small pockets of juice collecting on the meat and they look a little white, you can be sure the meat inside is medium.

Many home cooks like to use instant-read thermometers to determine when beef is done. We don't recommend this because we don't like to puncture our steaks until it's time to take knife and fork to them. If you would like to use an instant-read thermometer until you get the hang of our other testing methods, go ahead. After a while you won't need to poke one of these little things into your beautiful steaks. In the meantime, here are the temperatures for doneness:

EXTRA RARE	115°–120°F.
RARE	125°–130°F.
MEDIUM-RARE	135°–140°F.
MEDIUM	145°–150°F.
MEDIUM-WELL	155°–160°F.
WELL DONE	165°F.

(These temperatures apply to lamb as well, except lamb is rare at 140°F.)

EQUIPMENT

Whether you have a charcoal grill or a gas grill or plan to cook your steaks and chops under the broiler, you don't need much fancy equipment to be successful. The equipment you do have should be sturdy and of high quality so that it will last for years.

You will need long-handled tongs and spatulas to turn and move the meat. Never pierce meat with a fork, which only releases—and wastes—precious juices. Also stock the kitchen with good oven mitts, some thick pot holders (we like the silicone ones, too), wood and plastic cutting boards, and high-quality knives.

Buy knives you like to use and that feel good in your hand. Wooden or plastic handles are both fine, but the blade must run all the way through the handle, secured by rivets clearly visible in the handle. As a rule, expensive knives with high-carbon stainless-steel blades are the best choice.

Take care of your knives by washing and drying them by hand (never put them in the dishwasher) and storing them in a knife block or on a rack. Keep the blades sharp with frequent sharpening; keep the blades honed by running them over a steel every time you use them. Knives that are properly cared for will last a lifetime.

For some recipes in the book, you will need the usual assortment of heavy pans with lids, nonstick skillets, sauté pans, shallow glass dishes, mixing bowls, ovenproof ramekins, and soufflé dishes. Have some wooden spoons for mixing and wire whisks for smoothing out sauces and batters. We love the handheld immersion blender, an inexpensive appliance that smooths out food right in the cooking pot. Otherwise, our recipes are relatively easy to make with the equipment most families have on hand.

We're pleased that you want us to help you cook as we do. Steakhouses are an American institution, and with your enthusiasm and our know-how, you'll be eating as well as we do every day!

2

COCKTAILS AND THE FOOD WE EAT WITH THEM

COCKTAILS	COCKTAIL FOOD
Vodka Mortini	Smoked Salmon Pinwheels
Gin Mortini	Lump Crabmeat Canapés
Manhattan	Chicken Goujonettes
Rob Roy	Petite Lamb Chops
Morton's Cosmopolitan	Wild Mushroom Canapés with Brie
Palm Beach Infusion	Crab and Artichoke Dip with Parmesan Croutons
Espressotini	Petite Steak Sandwiches
Chocolatini	Morton's Mini Cheeseburgers
Appletini	Tempura-Style Shrimp
Key Lime Mortini	
Cadillac Margarita	
Mojito	
Tom Collins	
Sloe Gin Fizz	
Negroni	
Bellini	
Mimosa	
Kir Royale	

COCKTAILS AND WINE

The first night we opened our doors, more than twenty-five years ago, was during one of Chicago's biggest snowstorms, and so only a few guests straggled in. While the steaks were of course superb, it was the big, ice-cold martinis that kept everyone warm and happy. Not much has changed. Our guests may drink less nowadays, but they drink better, and the bar plays an important role at Morton's. Tylor Field III, our vice president of wine and spirits, is instrumental in seeing that the cocktail and wine programs run without a hitch.

Our most popular cocktail is the martini, and our most popular martini is a Grey Goose martini. We make our Twenty-fifth Anniversary vodka martini with Level vodka (made by Absolut) and call it a Mortini. Both are garnished with a colossal green olive stuffed with blue cheese (we buy Santa Barbara colossal olives and stuff them ourselves with Saga blue cheese). But we never have and never will put vermouth in our martinis.

Our guests frequently ask for specific brands. Our favorites, other than Grey Goose and Level vodka, are Bombay Sapphire gin, Ketel One Citroen vodka for our Cosmopolitans, Knob Creek bourbon, Jack Daniel's Tennessee whiskey, and a wide array of Scotch—we have a remarkable collection of single malts, all between ten and thirty-five years old, with Macallan being the benchmark. We also serve blended Scotch, of which Dewar's is the most popular.

Our wine selections are organized around the food, as yours should be. When you pair steak with wine, make the wine decision based on the fattiness of the steak. The fattier the steak, the better it will support a high-tannin wine. For example, I would pair a ribeye steak, which has a good amount of fat, with a cabernet sauvignon, which will cut the fat. I'd pair a leaner filet mignon with a lighter merlot. For these same reasons in reverse, I pair white wines with fish.

Cocktails should be made one drink at a time, so our recipes serve only one. The most important ingredient (after the alcohol) is the ice. If you can, make it with filtered or purified water to ensure that the drinks will taste as pure as possible.

A well-stocked bar has the right equipment. You don't need much, but a long cocktail spoon, a stainless-steel shaker with a glass pint glass, a cocktail strainer, a paring knife, and a small cutting board will make you a successful bartender.

We serve our martinis in 8-ounce glasses; our anniversary glasses are made of stainless steel and keep the contents very, very cold. For drinks other than martinis (and martinis include a wide spectrum of drinks), you will need old-fashioned glasses and highball glasses. Highball glasses hold three times as much as old-fashioned glasses and are for tall drinks such as a Tom Collins.

Try to serve wine in fine crystal glass stemware. We use Riedel's Cabernet glass, which is a 21-ounce, handblown, oversized glass—a dramatic glass. But of course, we never fill it.

VODKA MORTINI

SERVES 1

3 ounces vodka
1 pitted Santa Barbara colossal green olive (see Note)
1 teaspoon Saga blue cheese

1. Pour the vodka into a cocktail shaker filled with ice. Shake 15 times. Strain into a chilled martini glass.

2. Stuff the olive with the blue cheese. Garnish the Mortini with the olive.

Note: We buy Santa Barbara colossal green olives, which are outstanding, and hand-stuff them with cheese. If you find other giant pitted green olives, use them.

CELEBRITY CLIP

All the actors who have played James Bond have dined at Morton's. From Sean Connery to Pierce Brosnan, they seem to enjoy our steaks (and probably our extra-dry martinis!). I remember an evening when Roger Moore was in the Chicago Morton's. Before he ordered, he went from table to table signing autographs, shaking hands, and kissing all the ladies on the cheek. A very generous gesture.

GIN MORTINI

SERVES 1

3 ounces gin
1 pitted Santa Barbara colossal green olive (see Note, page 24)
1 teaspoon Saga blue cheese

1. Pour the gin into a cocktail shaker filled with ice. Shake 15 times. Strain into a chilled martini glass.

2. Stuff the olive with the blue cheese. Garnish the Mortini with the olive.

MANHATTAN

SERVES 1

3 ounces bourbon
1 tablespoon Monin cherry syrup
Splash of sweet vermouth
1 maraschino cherry, for garnish

1. Pour the bourbon, cherry syrup, and vermouth into a cocktail shaker filled with ice. Shake 15 times.

2. Strain into a chilled martini glass and garnish with the cherry.

ROB ROY

SERVES 1

$2\frac{1}{2}$ ounces Scotch
1 ounce sweet vermouth
Lemon twist, for garnish

1. Combine the Scotch and vermouth in a cocktail shaker filled with ice cubes. Shake vigorously 15 times.

2. Strain into a chilled martini glass and garnish with the lemon twist.

MORTON'S COSMOPOLITAN

SERVES 1

2 ounces Ketel One Citroen vodka
½ ounce Cointreau
½ ounce Grand Marnier
1 tablespoon Ocean Spray cranberry purée, or 2 tablespoons frozen Ocean Spray
cranberry juice concentrate, undiluted (see Note)
Juice of 1 lime wedge
1 slender lime wedge, for garnish

1. Pour the vodka, Cointreau, Grand Marnier, cranberry purée, and lime juice into a cocktail shaker filled with ice. Shake 15 times. Strain into a chilled martini glass.

2. Garnish with the lime wedge.

Note: Ocean Spray cranberry purée is not always easily available to the general public, since most of it goes straight to restaurants and bars, probably because the demand for it is not high among consumers. It's sold in some liquor stores, so if you can find it, use it. Otherwise, undiluted cranberry juice concentrate is a good substitute, although you need twice as much concentrate as purée, as noted in the recipe.

PALM BEACH INFUSION

SERVES 1

3 ounces Infused Vodka (recipe follows)
1 tablespoon pineapple juice
1 tablespoon Monin cherry syrup
1 fresh mint leaf, for garnish

1. Pour the vodka, pineapple juice, and cherry syrup into a cocktail shaker filled with ice cubes. Shake 15 times.

2. Strain into a chilled martini glass and garnish with the mint leaf.

INFUSED VODKA
MAKES ABOUT ½ LITER

1 pineapple, peeled, cored, and thinly sliced
½ liter vodka
4 to 5 fresh mint sprigs (small bunch)

1. Put the pineapple slices in a large, non-reactive jar or other container with a lid. Pour the vodka over the fruit and add the mint sprigs. Cover tightly and set aside at room temperature for 24 hours.

2. Strain the vodka and discard the fruit. Refrigerate for up to 10 days.

ESPRESSOTINI

SERVES 1

> 2 ounces Stolichnaya Vanil vodka
> 1 ounce Kahlúa
> 3 tablespoons (1 demitasse cup)
>   brewed and chilled Illy espresso or
>   other brewed espresso
> 1 teaspoon sugar
> 3 espresso beans, for garnish

1. Combine the vodka, Kahlúa, espresso, and sugar in a cocktail shaker filled with ice cubes. Shake vigorously 25 times to create froth.

2. Strain into a chilled martini glass and garnish with espresso beans on top of the froth.

CELEBRITY CLIP

When we opened our sixth Washington, D.C.–area Morton's in Bethesda, Maryland, the Washington Redskins hosted a charity event at the new restaurant. This was to benefit the Redskins Charitable Foundation, founded by team owner Daniel Snyder to raise awareness of the needs of D.C.-area youth. Both Snyder and Joe Gibbs, the Redskins' head coach, are regulars at Morton's, so it was not surprising that on another occasion players showed up at the Georgetown and Reston, Virginia, restaurants to act as celebrity bartenders. Their generous tips all went to the foundation.

CHOCOLATINI

SERVES 1

2 tablespoons Hershey's Shell Topping
2 to 3 teaspoons chocolate sugar (see Note)
1 orange slice
1½ ounces Van Gogh Dutch Chocolate vodka
2 tablespoons half-and-half
½ ounce chocolate liqueur
½ ounce dark crème de cacao

1. Pour the topping into a chilled martini glass. Swirl the glass, angling it so that the topping covers the bottom of the glass and comes about halfway up the sides. The topping will harden quickly on contact with the cold glass. Return the glass to the refrigerator until ready to use, to give the chocolate time to set.

2. Spread the chocolate sugar on a small flat plate or similar surface. Run the orange slice around the rim of the glass to moisten it. Dip the rim in the sugar to coat it.

3. Pour the vodka, half-and-half, liqueur, and crème de cacao into a cocktail shaker filled with ice cubes. Shake 15 times. Strain into the martini glass and serve.

Note: We buy premade chocolate sugar, a mixture of granulated sugar and semisweet chocolate. If you can't find it, mix about 1 teaspoon sugar with 1 teaspoon finely grated semisweet or bittersweet chocolate.

APPLETINI

SERVES 1

1 teaspoon ground cinnamon
1 teaspoon sugar
1 lemon wedge
1 tablespoon Monin green apple syrup (see Note)
2 ounces Absolut Citron vodka
1½ ounces DeKuyper Sour Apple Pucker schnapps
1 tablespoon lemonade

1. Spread the cinnamon and sugar on a flat plate or similar surface. Rub the lemon wedge around the rim of a chilled martini glass. Dip the rim in the cinnamon sugar. Pour the apple syrup into the glass.

2. Pour the vodka, schnapps, and lemonade into a cocktail shaker filled with ice cubes. Shake 15 times. Strain slowly into the martini glass so that the martini floats on top of the syrup.

Note: Apple syrup is sold in liquor stores and some specialty markets.

KEY LIME MORTINI

SERVES 1

2 teaspoons finely crushed graham crackers
1 lime wedge
2 ounces Licor 43 (see Note)
1 ounce Charbay vodka
1 tablespoon half-and-half
1 teaspoon fresh lime juice

1. Spread the graham crackers on a flat plate or similar surface. Rub the lime wedge around the rim of a chilled martini glass. Dip the rim in the graham crackers to coat.

2. Pour the Licor 43, vodka, half-and-half, and lime juice into a cocktail shaker filled with ice cubes. Shake 15 times. Strain into the martini glass.

Note: Licor 43 (Cuarenta y Tres) is a Spanish liqueur made with forty-three ingredients. It has citrus, herbal, and vanilla notes and is available in liquor stores.

CADILLAC MARGARITA

SERVES 1

2 ounces tequila
Juice of $\frac{1}{2}$ **lime**
1 ounce Cointreau
$\frac{1}{2}$ **ounce Grand Marnier**
1 tablespoon bottled margarita mix (we use Daily's)
Margarita salt (optional)**, for salting glass**
2 lime wedges

1. Pour the tequila, lime juice, Cointreau, Grand Marnier, and margarita mix into a cocktail shaker filled with ice cubes. Shake 15 times.

2. If using the salt, spread it on a plate. Rub one of the lime wedges around the rim of a chilled martini glass and dip it into the salt.

3. Strain the margarita into the glass, squeeze the juice of the remaining lime wedge into the cocktail, and serve.

MOJITO

SERVES 1

3 fresh mint leaves
1 tablespoon Simple Syrup (recipe follows)
1½ ounces light Bacardi or Havana Club rum
2 tablespoons fresh lime juice
Club soda

1. In a small bowl, mix two of the mint leaves with the syrup. With the back of a spoon, press the leaves to release their essential oils. Pour into a cocktail shaker filled with ice cubes.

2. Add the rum and lime juice. Shake 5 times. Strain into a highball glass filled with a few ice cubes. Pour in the club soda to fill and garnish with the remaining mint leaf.

SIMPLE SYRUP
MAKES ABOUT 1 CUP

1 cup sugar
1 cup water

1. In a small, heavy saucepan, mix the sugar with the water. Bring to a boil over medium-high heat, stirring, for about 1 minute, or until the sugar dissolves and the syrup is clear.

2. Remove the pan from the heat and let the syrup cool to room temperature. Transfer to a glass jar with a tight-fitting lid and refrigerate. The syrup can be refrigerated for up to 1 month.

TOM COLLINS

SERVES 1

1½ ounces gin
2 tablespoons fresh lemon juice
2 tablespoons Simple Syrup (recipe opposite)
Club soda
1 cherry, for garnish
1 orange slice, for garnish

1. Pour the gin, lemon juice, and syrup into a cocktail shaker. Shake 5 times.

2. Pour into a highball glass filled with a few ice cubes. Add the club soda to fill and garnish with the cherry and orange slice.

CELEBRITY CLIP

Jackie Gleason was a cool guy who liked our food a lot. He always ordered his cocktails without ice, and would ask us to bring him a Coke in the same glass when his wife arrived! We don't think she was fooled for a minute, but the two of them always had a great time at the restaurant.

SLOE GIN FIZZ

SERVES 1

1 ounce sloe gin
1 ounce gin
1½ tablespoons fresh lemon juice
2 tablespoons Simple Syrup (page 34)
Club soda
1 orange slice, for garnish
1 maraschino cherry, for garnish

1. Pour the gins, lemon juice, and syrup into a cocktail shaker. Shake 5 times.

2. Pour into a highball glass filled with a few ice cubes. Add the club soda to fill and garnish with the orange slice and cherry.

NEGRONI

SERVES 1

1 ounce gin
1 ounce sweet vermouth
1 ounce Campari
1 lemon twist, for garnish

1. Pour the gin, vermouth, and Campari into a cocktail shaker. Shake 15 times.

2. Pour into an old-fashioned glass filled with ice cubes and garnish with the lemon twist.

CADILLAC
MARGARITA

BELLINI

MOJITO

NEGRONI

BELLINI

SERVES 1

1 teaspoon peach sugar or granulated sugar (see Note)
1 peach wedge
2 tablespoons commercial Finest Call peach purée (see Note)
4 ounces chilled Blanc de Blanc sparkling wine or champagne

1. Spread the sugar on a flat plate or similar surface. Rub the peach wedge around the rim of a champagne flute to moisten it. Dip the rim in the sugar to coat.

2. Pour the peach purée into the glass. Slowly pour in the wine and mix gently until well blended.

Note: Peach sugar and peach purée may be available at liquor stores and specialty markets. If not, substitute 2 tablespoons of very ripe, mashed peach.

MIMOSA

SERVES 1

¼ cup chilled fresh orange juice
4 ounces chilled champagne

1. Pour the orange juice into a champagne flute.

2. Add the champagne and serve.

KIR ROYALE

SERVES 1

½ ounce crème de cassis
4 ounces chilled champagne

1. Pour the crème de cassis into a champagne flute.

2. Add the champagne and serve.

SMOKED SALMON PINWHEELS

Buy good-quality smoked salmon from a gourmet store or in a plastic package at the supermarket. When you buy the packaged salmon it is already sliced, so you need only to lift the slices from the package and overlap them to form a rectangle. The slices will stick together nicely, making it easy to form them into a roll.

MAKES 20 PINWHEELS

4 ounces cream cheese, softened
1½ teaspoons finely chopped fresh dill
5 ounces thinly sliced smoked salmon
5 slices very thin white bread

1. Put the softened cream cheese into a small bowl. Add the dill and mix well.

2. Lay slices of smoked salmon on a work surface, overlapping the slices to form a long, rectangular shape about 6 by 8 inches. Trim the edges to square the rectangle. Spread the cream cheese over the salmon in an even layer about ⅛ inch thick. Make sure to cover the salmon completely with the cheese. Using a knife to lift the short end of the rectangle, roll the salmon over and continue to roll to the other end. Transfer the roll to a baking sheet and cover with plastic wrap. Refrigerate for at least 2 hours.

3. Preheat the broiler.

4. Lay out the bread on a broiling pan. Broil each side for 1 to 2 minutes, or until golden brown. Trim the crusts off the bread to create a square. Cut each slice of bread from corner to corner into four triangles.

5. Remove the salmon roll from the refrigerator. Cut the roll crosswise into slices about ⅜ inch thick. Put one salmon slice on each triangle of toast. Let the salmon rolls and toast reach cool room temperature to serve. Serve immediately or refrigerate until ready to serve.

LUMP CRABMEAT CANAPÉS

These canapés couldn't be easier to make. Just be sure to handle the crabmeat with care. If you buy quality lump meat, you won't have to worry too much about finding small pieces of shell because these large lumps are usually very clean.

MAKES 16 CANAPÉS

$\frac{1}{2}$ **pound lump crabmeat**
$\frac{1}{4}$ **cup Mustard-Mayonnaise Sauce** (page 222)
4 slices very thin white bread, toasted
4 leaves romaine lettuce
4 large green olives, pitted and thinly sliced

1. Pick through the crabmeat to remove any bits of shell. Put the crabmeat into a clean kitchen towel. Gently squeeze to remove any excess liquid.

2. In a small bowl, gently mix the crabmeat with 3 tablespoons of the Mustard-Mayonnaise Sauce. The lumps will break a little but the mixture should not be smooth. Set aside.

3. Spread a thin layer of the remaining 1 tablespoon of Mustard-Mayonnaise Sauce onto each slice of toasted bread. Lay the lettuce leaves flat on the countertop. Put a slice of bread, mayonnaise side down, on top of each lettuce leaf. Cut the crusts off the bread and trim the lettuce leaves to the size of the bread.

4. Flip the bread over. Cut each slice into four triangles. Top each with about 1 heaping teaspoon of the crabmeat, garnish with a few olive slices, and serve.

CHICKEN GOUJONETTES

These are one of my favorite appetizers both at Morton's and at home. True, they are nothing more than glorified chicken fingers, but the fresh bread crumbs make them nice and crisp. Be sure the oil is hot enough when you deep-fry so that the coating and chicken cook quickly and the oil doesn't seep into the meat.

MAKES 24 TO 30 GOUJONETTES

One 1-pound loaf unsliced firm white bread
Salt and freshly ground black pepper
1½ pounds boneless, skinless chicken breasts, trimmed
⅔ cup all-purpose flour
4 large eggs
2 quarts flavorless vegetable oil, such as canola or safflower
1½ cups Mustard-Mayonnaise Sauce (page 222)

1. Trim the crust off the bread and cut the bread into large chunks. Put the bread in the bowl of a food processor fitted with a metal blade and process to fine bread crumbs. Season with salt and pepper to taste. You will have about 3 cups of bread crumbs.

2. Slice the chicken into 4- to 6-inch-long strips about ½ inch wide. You should have 24 to 30 strips.

3. Spread the flour on a plate. Whisk the eggs with 2 tablespoons of water in a shallow bowl. Spread the bread crumbs on another plate. Line up these ingredients in a row.

4. Coat the chicken strips on both sides with flour and shake off any excess. Dip in the egg wash, and let the excess drip off. Roll the chicken strips in the bread crumbs. Set aside on a parchment-lined baking sheet.

5. Pour the oil into a deep-fryer or a deep, heavy saucepan. Heat the oil over medium-high heat until a deep-frying thermometer registers 350°F.

6. Using tongs, submerge the chicken strips, one at a time, into the hot oil, or use a frying basket, making sure not to crowd the chicken. Deep-fry for 3 to 4 minutes, or until the goujonettes are golden brown and cooked through. Remove with a slotted spoon and transfer to paper towels to drain. Repeat with the remaining chicken strips. Serve immediately with the Mustard-Mayonnaise Sauce.

PETITE LAMB CHOPS

I can't help referring to these little chops as both fun and charming—some people call them "lollipop chops." One or two bites, which is about all these are, can make even the most ardent beef eater develop a weakness for lamb! They can be served at a cocktail party, or a few can take the place of a main course.

MAKES 18 CHOPS

Eighteen 2-ounce baby lamb chops, $\frac{1}{2}$ to $\frac{1}{4}$ inch thick
   (cut from New Zealand racks of baby lamb or young lamb)
2 teaspoons seasoned salt
$1\frac{1}{2}$ tablespoons minced garlic
$1\frac{1}{2}$ tablespoons fresh oregano leaves
Olive oil

1. Season the lamb chops on both sides with the seasoned salt. Gently press the garlic and oregano into the meat. Transfer the chops to a glass baking dish or bowl large enough to hold all of them. Pour in enough olive oil to cover the lamb chops. Cover with plastic wrap and refrigerate for at least 5 hours or overnight.

2. Remove the lamb chops from the refrigerator and let them come to room temperature.

3. Heat a large sauté pan over high heat. Lift five or six lamb chops from the dish, let the excess oil drip back into the bowl, and then lay the chops in the hot pan without crowding. Adjust the heat if it seems too hot; you don't want to burn the garlic and oregano. Cook for about 30 seconds, or until the chops are browned but the oregano is not burned. Turn the chops over and cook for 30 to 45 seconds for rare meat. Watch the meat closely as it may cook in less time depending on the thickness of the meat and the heat of the pan. Remove the pan from the heat. Transfer the chops to a plate and keep warm in a low (250°F.) oven. Repeat with the remaining lamb chops. Serve immediately.

WILD MUSHROOM CANAPÉS WITH BRIE

For these, we mix three different kinds of mushrooms. If you can't find the mushrooms we call for, use others. Even white mushrooms work well, although they are best if mixed with shiitakes or others for some variety. Brie cheese, which softens at room temperature, must be frozen before it can be grated. If you want to grate it ahead of time, return the grated cheese to the freezer until you are ready to melt it. It softens quickly at room temperature, especially when grated.

MAKES 20 CANAPÉS

1 French baguette, about 14 inches long and 3 inches wide
4 ounces portobello mushrooms (about 2 medium mushrooms)
3 ounces shiitake mushrooms (about 6 mushrooms)
4 ounces cremini mushrooms (about 10 mushrooms)
6 tablespoons Garlic Butter (page 224)
4 ounces unpeeled Brie cheese, frozen

1. Preheat the oven to 450°F.

2. Trim the ends off the baguettes and save for another use, such as bread crumbs. Cut the baguettes on an angle into twenty $\frac{1}{4}$-inch-thick slices. Toast the bread in the oven in a single layer on a baking sheet for 4 to 5 minutes, until light golden brown.

3. Twist the stems off the portobello and shiitake mushrooms and discard. Trim the stems from the cremini and discard. Using a small paring knife, scrape the underside of the portobellos clean of dark gills.

4. Slice all the mushrooms into $\frac{1}{4}$-inch-wide strips, and then chop them into $\frac{1}{2}$- to 1-inch-long pieces. You will have about 4 cups of roughly chopped pieces.

5. In a large sauté pan, melt the Garlic Butter over medium-high heat. Add the mushrooms and sauté for 4 to 5 minutes, or until softened. The mushrooms will cook down to about $1\frac{1}{3}$ cups.

6. Lay the bread out on the baking sheet. Top each slice of toast with 1 tablespoon of the mushroom mixture.

7. Using a cheese grater, coarsely grate the frozen Brie so that you have about 1 cup. Sprinkle the grated Brie over the mushroom mixture and bake for about 5 minutes, or until the Brie melts. Serve immediately.

CRAB AND ARTICHOKE DIP
WITH PARMESAN CROUTONS

The blending of crab and artichokes in a creamy sauce perfectly seasoned with a few dashes of Tabasco and Worcestershire can't be beat. This is great for casual get-togethers, yet the crabmeat dresses it up so that it is also welcome at elegant cocktail parties.

MAKES ABOUT 3 CUPS DIP AND 16 CROUTONS

$1\frac{1}{2}$ teaspoons unsalted butter
$\frac{1}{4}$ cup minced Spanish onion (1 small onion)
8 ounces cream cheese
$\frac{1}{4}$ cup half-and-half
$1\frac{1}{2}$ teaspoons drained prepared horseradish
$\frac{1}{2}$ teaspoon Tabasco sauce
$\frac{1}{2}$ teaspoon Worcestershire sauce
$\frac{1}{2}$ teaspoon Old Bay Seasoning
1 cup sliced artichoke hearts, frozen or canned,
   packed in brine and drained ($5\frac{1}{5}$ ounces)
4 ounces lump crabmeat, picked through to remove any shell
3 tablespoons grated Parmesan cheese
$\frac{1}{4}$ cup extra-virgin olive oil
Sixteen $\frac{1}{2}$-inch-thick slices baguette
   (from a standard $2\frac{1}{2}$-inch-diameter baguette)
Curly-leaf parsley sprigs, for garnish

1. Preheat the oven to 450°F.

2. In a saucepan, melt the butter over medium heat. Add the onion and sauté for 3 minutes, or until softened but not browned. Add the cream cheese and cook, stirring frequently, for 2 to 3 minutes, or until the cream cheese melts. Add the half-and-half and stir to combine with the cream cheese. Add the horseradish, Tabasco and Worcestershire sauces, and Old Bay Seasoning. Stir well. Fold in the artichoke hearts. Once they are added, gently fold in the crabmeat. Take care to keep the lumps of crabmeat as whole as possible. You will have about 3 cups.

3. Transfer to a 9- to 10-inch pie plate or similar shallow ovenproof dish. Sprinkle 2 tablespoons of the Parmesan over the dip and bake for 9 to 10 minutes, or until the cheese is lightly browned and the dip is lightly bubbling around the edges. Remove from the oven and set aside, covered, to keep warm.

4. Turn off the oven and preheat the broiler.

5. Pour the olive oil into a shallow dish. Dip one side of each baguette slice in the oil and put on a broiler tray, oiled side up. Sprinkle the remaining Parmesan over the croutons. Broil the croutons for about 45 seconds about 2 inches from the heat, or until golden brown on top. Watch them carefully.

6. Garnish the dip with the parsley and serve with the croutons.

PETITE STEAK SANDWICHES

The key to these easy sandwiches is very soft rolls and very tender meat. This makes them easy to eat out of hand. Filet is the softest, tenderest of steaks, which is why we use it here. In the restaurants, we use up the ends of the filets, which we don't serve as part of our main-course dishes. You might choose instead to buy a whole filet for your sandwiches, or you may have some narrow ends stashed in the freezer, cut from a whole filet from another meal.

MAKES 18 SANDWICHES

18 ounces beef tenderloin, tail or end
Seasoned salt
18 finger sandwich rolls with sesame seeds or
   any small finger roll, each about 3 inches long and 1 inch wide
2 tablespoons Mustard-Mayonnaise Sauce (page 222)

1. Preheat the broiler and position the rack 2 to 3 inches from the heating element.

2. Lightly season the tenderloin with seasoned salt. Arrange on a broiler tray and tuck the thin end portions under, if necessary, to prevent them from cooking too fast. Broil for 6 to 7 minutes, turning once, for medium-rare, or longer depending on the thickness and desired doneness.

3. Meanwhile, slice the rolls in half. Place the rolls, cut side up, on a baking sheet. Toast under the broiler for about 2 minutes, or until lightly browned. Turn them over and toast for 1 to 2 minutes longer, or until lightly browned and heated through.

4. Spread the rolls with the Mustard-Mayonnaise Sauce. Slice the tenderloin across the grain into 18 pieces. Put a slice of tenderloin on the bottom half of each roll. Top with the other half of the roll and serve.

MORTON'S MINI CHEESEBURGERS

I have never met anyone who didn't love these little burgers, which are perfect for a casual outdoor party. Just one of these satisfies a craving for a cheeseburger, but it's easy to eat two or three at a time. Use the best ground sirloin you can find, preferably from a butcher who will grind it for you or from a store that grinds all their meat on the premises. Ask for medium-grind meat, not fine-grind, which can be mushy. Don't overcook these little cheeseburgers; they are juicy bites of beef heaven!

MAKES 12 MINI CHEESEBURGERS

2 pounds ground sirloin (see Note)
6 tablespoons tomato juice
2 large eggs
$1^{1}/_{2}$ teaspoons salt
$^{1}/_{2}$ teaspoon freshly ground black pepper
12 mini hamburger buns or small, soft dinner rolls,
    each about $2^{1}/_{2}$ inches in diameter, split in half
6 ounces Cheddar cheese, cut into thin slices
    about the size of the burgers
12 leaves iceberg lettuce, each about 1 inch
    larger than the buns
12 slices plum or other ripe tomato,
    about the same size as the burgers
12 slices red onion, each about $^{1}/_{8}$ inch thick
Ketchup, for serving
Mustard, for serving

1. Preheat the broiler. Position the broiler tray about 2 inches from the heat source.

2. In a mixing bowl, combine the sirloin, tomato juice, eggs, salt, and pepper. Use your hands or a wooden spoon to mix thoroughly but gently. Divide the meat into 12 equal portions and form into hamburger patties.

3. Remove the broiler tray from the broiler and arrange the buns, cut side down, on the tray. Toast the buns under the broiler for about 30 seconds on each side, or until lightly browned. Be careful that the buns do not get too browned. Remove the buns and reserve.

4. Arrange the burgers on the broiler tray and broil for 3 to $3^{1}/_{2}$ minutes. Turn over and broil for 3 to $3^{1}/_{2}$ minutes longer for medium. Lay the cheese on top of the burgers during the last $1^{1}/_{2}$ minutes of cooking. (For medium-rare, broil the hamburgers for $2^{1}/_{2}$ to 3 minutes on each side; for well done, broil for about 4 minutes on each side.)

5. Put the cheeseburgers on the buns and garnish each with lettuce, tomato, and onion. Secure with a toothpick, if it makes serving easier. Serve the cheeseburgers with ketchup and mustard on the side.

Note: We use ground sirloin with an 80:20 ratio of lean beef to fat. Try to find beef with a similar ratio for the juiciest burgers.

TEMPURA-STYLE SHRIMP

Who doesn't love fried shrimp? When shrimp is coated with a light batter that puffs up in the fryer, the results are nothing short of spectacular. For this recipe I like to use peanut oil, which gets nice and hot; also, the very subtle peanut flavor marries well with the Asian flavors in the batter. Don't crowd the pan when you fry the shrimp, and be sure to let the oil return to its hot temperature between batches. A little patience pays off big time!

SERVES 6

36 large or jumbo shrimp (21/25 count or,
    if possible, 16/20 count; see Note)
1 large egg yolk
2 tablespoons roasted sesame oil
2 teaspoons wasabi powder
Salt and freshly ground black pepper
⅔ cup all-purpose flour
¼ cup cornstarch
1 cup panko bread crumbs (see Note)
Peanut oil or another vegetable oil,
    such as canola or safflower, for frying
1¼ cups Cocktail Sauce (page 225)
3 lemons, halved, for garnish
12 curly-leaf parsley sprigs, for garnish

1. Peel, devein, and butterfly the shrimp. Pat dry with paper towels.

2. In a large mixing bowl, stir the egg yolk, sesame oil, and wasabi powder with 1 cup of cold water. Season to taste with salt and pepper and mix well.

3. In a small bowl, whisk together the flour and cornstarch. Sprinkle over the liquid, constantly whisking until incorporated. Put the bowl in a larger bowl filled with ice cubes to keep the batter cold and help it thicken.

4. Spread the bread crumbs on a large plate. Dip each shrimp into the batter, letting any excess drip back into the bowl. Dip immediately into the bread crumbs, pressing down to coat completely. Set aside on a parchment-lined baking sheet.

5. Pour the oil into a heavy saucepan or high-sided skillet to a depth of 3 inches. Heat over high heat until shimmering and a deep-frying thermometer registers 375°F. Fry the shrimp in batches for about 3 minutes, or until golden brown. Lift from the oil with tongs and drain on paper towels.

6. To serve, place six shrimp on each of six plates and spoon Cocktail Sauce on the plate next to them. Garnish with lemon halves and parsley.

Notes: Shrimp are sold by the pound. The count indicates how many shrimp of a certain size are needed to weigh 1 pound. For example, shrimp sold as "16/20 count" are larger than those sold as "21/25 count."

Panko are light, delicate, Japanese-style bread crumbs sold in many supermarkets, often in the Asian food aisle.

CELEBRITY CLIP

Frank Sinatra showed up at Morton's about six weeks after we opened. It was a cold Friday in February, and we were doing a respectable business, but did not expect a celebrity of Sinatra's stature to walk in the door. The press got wind of it and the next day our phones rang off the hook, with people calling for reservations. We called Raki Mehra, who at that time worked at Arnie's, the restaurant Arnie Morton and I had opened a few years earlier. We needed Raki to help with the increased traffic. Since that day, Raki has been at our State Street (the original) Morton's, where he is the general manager and maître d'.

3

APPETIZERS

Steakhouse Shrimp Cocktail

Sea Scallops Wrapped with Bacon

Smoked Salmon with All the Trimmings

Oysters on the Half Shell

Broiled Sea Scallops with Apricot Chutney

Belgian Endive with Blue Cheese

Chicken Liver Pâté

Mushroom Caps with Deviled Crab

Baked Crab Cakes with Mustard-Mayonnaise Sauce

Grilled Asparagus with Roasted Red Pepper

STEAKHOUSE SHRIMP COCKTAIL

There is no question that the shrimp cocktail has timeless appeal. Here we suggest using the biggest shrimp you can find and call for 21/25 or 16/20 count, which simply means there are 21 to 25 shrimp, or 16 to 20 shrimp, per pound. Obviously the smaller number means bigger shrimp.

SERVES 6

2 to 3 bay leaves
2 lemons, halved
24 large or jumbo shrimp (21/25 count, or, if possible, 16/20 count)**, deveined**
1¹⁄₂ cups Cocktail Sauce (page 225)

1. Fill a large saucepan with water. Add the bay leaves, squeeze in the juice from one of the lemons, and add the unsqueezed lemon halves. Bring to a boil over high heat, reduce the heat to medium, and simmer for 30 minutes.

2. Add the shrimp to the simmering water so that they are completely immersed. Bring the water to a boil and cook the shrimp for 4 to 5 minutes if thawed and for about 8 minutes if frozen. Drain in a colander and cover with crushed ice to chill. Discard the lemon halves and bay leaves.

3. Remove the shrimp from the ice and put the chilled shrimp in a container. Cover and refrigerate for 1 to 2 hours.

4. Serve the chilled shrimp with the Cocktail Sauce.

SEA SCALLOPS WRAPPED WITH BACON

Kevin Weinert, our senior vice president of operations, came up with this dish a number of years ago after seeing something similar in one of James Beard's cookbooks. Beard served oysters wrapped in bacon and called them Angels on Horseback. Our name may not be as whimsical, but these are just as delicious. We like the Apricot Chutney with both of our scallop dishes. Buy fresh scallops, as described on page 64.

SERVES 6

18 slices bacon (about 1 pound)
18 jumbo sea scallops (1¼ to 1½ pounds),
    side tendons removed
6 tablespoons unsalted butter, melted
18 to 24 large leaves fresh spinach,
    stemmed, rinsed, and patted dry
6 tablespoons Apricot Chutney (page 219)
3 lemons, halved

1. Preheat the oven to 450°F.

2. Soak six 6-inch-long bamboo skewers in cold water for 20 minutes.

3. Place a wire rack on top of a baking sheet, and spread the bacon out on the rack. Bake for 10 minutes, or until the bacon is lightly browned but still pliable enough to wrap around the scallops. (Alternatively, cook the bacon in two skillets over medium heat until lightly browned but still pliable.) Drain the bacon on paper towels. If not using immediately, wrap it in a moist paper towel; this keeps it soft.

4. Wrap a slice of bacon around each scallop. Thread the scallops through the bacon onto the skewers, leaving ½ inch between each scallop. There should be 3 scallops on each skewer. Cook immediately or cover and refrigerate until ready to use.

5. Pour the butter into a 9 × 13-inch ovenproof dish large enough to hold the skewers in a single layer. Put the skewers in the dish and rotate in the butter to evenly coat the scallops, then lay the skewers flat in the pan. Roast the scallops for 4 minutes. Turn and roast for about 4 minutes longer, or until the scallops are opaque and the bacon crisps up.

6. Arrange three or four spinach leaves on each of six small plates. Carefully slide the scallops from the skewers using a fork or small, blunt knife, and put three scallops on each plate on top of the leaves. Spoon a tablespoon of chutney beside the scallops. Serve garnished with the lemon halves.

CELEBRITY CLIP

Morton's Steakhouse in Las Vegas is just off the Strip at the corner of Paradise and Flamingo, and it's no surprise that we attract a lot of business travelers who come to Vegas for conventions and conferences. When the Consumer Electronics show is in town we have come to expect a familiar face at the restaurant: Microsoft chairman Bill Gates.

SMOKED SALMON WITH ALL THE TRIMMINGS

The key here is to use the best possible fish. (We have been buying smoked Pacific salmon from the same Washington State purveyor for about twenty years. I can't imagine better American smoked salmon anywhere.) Slice it as thin as you can, using a long, thin slicing knife that you can work back and forth along the side of the fish. Better yet, ask the fishmonger to slice it for you. You may not have the option of working with a fishmonger, since much of the smoked salmon available today is sold in vacuum-packed plastic. Luckily, these products are generally very good.

SERVES 6

> **1 cup prepared horseradish**
> **1 cup finely chopped white onion**
> **About 1 cup capers, drained** (3½-ounce jar)
> **3 lemons, halved**
> **1½- to 2-pound piece smoked salmon,**
>   **or 1½ to 2 pounds sliced smoked salmon**
> **Curly-leaf parsley**
> **Toast points** (optional; see Note)

1. Drain the horseradish through a fine-mesh sieve for 1 to 2 minutes, pushing gently on the horseradish with the back of a spoon. Place the drained horseradish in a small bowl.

2. Put the onion, capers, and lemon halves in separate small bowls.

3. Using a long slicing knife, slice the salmon as thin as you can. Make sure the knife is very sharp.

4. Serve the salmon on a marble board or platter with the horseradish, onion, capers, lemons, parsley, and toast points, if using.

   Note: To make toast points, lightly toast slices of thin-sliced bread, trim the crusts, and cut the bread in half on the diagonal to make triangles.

OYSTERS ON THE HALF SHELL

The secret to this recipe is to use the freshest and best oysters you can find, preferably local oysters or ones shipped in daily to a good fish store. Make sure all are tightly closed and discard those that are not. The fishmonger will shuck them for you, which will make your life easier, but if you take this route be sure to eat the oysters in an hour or two. Ask the fishmonger for shaved or crushed ice—he probably will give you some for very little or no charge. Carry the oysters home packed on the ice and then, once home, store them on the shaved ice in the refrigerator. Whether the oysters are shucked or still closed, store them in the shells, cup side down.

SERVES 6

36 oysters
About 2 quarts crushed ice
3 lemons, halved
1$\frac{1}{2}$ cups Cocktail Sauce (page 225)
$\frac{3}{4}$ cup drained prepared horseradish
Tabasco or other hot pepper sauce

1. Thoroughly scrub the oysters with a brush. Using an oyster knife, shuck the oysters. Loosen each oyster from the shell and then cut off the muscle from the bottom of the oyster. Leave the oyster in the bottom shell. Discard the top shells.

2. Spread the crushed ice on a large platter so that it's about $\frac{1}{2}$ inch deep. Arrange the oysters in their bottom shells on the crushed ice. Serve with the lemons, Cocktail Sauce, horseradish, and Tabasco sauce on the side.

BROILED SEA SCALLOPS WITH APRICOT CHUTNEY

The biggest mistake anyone can make when preparing scallops is to overcook them. Try to cook them just until they are translucent in the center, or medium done. Otherwise, they might taste rubbery. Buy large, fresh scallops without any added preserving solution. Known as dry scallops, these fresh scallops are never bright white but instead are creamy to pale pink.

SERVES 6

1 tablespoon unsalted butter, melted
12 jumbo sea scallops (about 1 pound), **side tendons removed**
12 large leaves fresh spinach, stemmed, rinsed, and patted dry
3 to 4 teaspoons Apricot Chutney (page 219)

1. Preheat the broiler and position the rack 2 to 3 inches from the heating element.

2. Lightly brush a small baking sheet with a thin layer of the butter and spread the scallops on the baking sheet. Broil the scallops for 3 to 5 minutes, or until golden brown. Turn them once during cooking for even browning.

3. Crisscross two spinach leaves on each of six small plates and put two scallops on top of the leaves. Top each scallop with a generous $1/4$ teaspoon of Apricot Chutney. Serve immediately.

BELGIAN ENDIVE WITH BLUE CHEESE

The bitterness of the endive and the pungency of the blue cheese play off each other in this classic hors d'oeuvre. Don't separate and trim the leaves of the endive until you are ready to fill and serve them; the snipped ends will turn brown if exposed to the air for too long. Use your favorite type of blue cheese; we like Saga blue, although a good gorgonzola or American Maytag would be excellent.

SERVES 6

10 to 11 ounces blue cheese, crumbled
⅔ cup mayonnaise
3 large heads Belgian endive, each 9 to 10 ounces
About 3 tablespoons snipped fresh chives, for garnish

1. In a small mixing bowl and using a fork, mix the blue cheese and mayonnaise.

2. Separate the leaves of the endive so that you have 30 to 36 leaves. Trim off the bottom ¼ inch of the leaves.

3. To serve, spoon about 2 teaspoons of the blue cheese mixture into the white, snipped end of each leaf. Garnish with the snipped chives.

CHICKEN LIVER PÂTÉ

If you are a fan of pâté, you'll surely love this one. Chicken liver pâté is a classic, and this traditional technique pays off with a rich, luxurious pâté that can be served as a first course or put on croutons and passed at a cocktail party. It takes patience to make, but none of the steps is difficult on its own. Just be sure you have plenty of room in the refrigerator before you start.

SERVES 6; MAKES 1 LOAF

FOR THE PÂTÉ

2 pounds chicken livers
2 tablespoons Clarified Butter (page 231)
¾ cup finely chopped shallots (about 3 shallots)
3 tablespoons minced garlic
1 tablespoon finely chopped fresh thyme leaves, plus 3 to 4 whole sprigs
¼ cup plus 1 tablespoon (2½ ounces) Port wine
¾ pound (3 sticks) unsalted butter, softened
⅛ teaspoon ground allspice
Salt and freshly ground black pepper

TO SERVE

Eighteen ¼- to ½-inch-wide slices baguette, cut on an angle
6 tablespoons whole-grain mustard
30 cornichons
6 watercress sprigs

1. Remove all the connective tissue and fat from the chicken livers. Put half of the cleaned livers in a mesh colander or similar strainer with a handle.

2. Bring a large pot of salted water to a boil. Reduce the heat so that the water is gently boiling. Submerge the colander holding half the livers in the boiling water and cook, uncovered, for 5 to 7 minutes to blanch, or until, when sliced, a liver is slightly pink in the center and not raw. The time depends on the size of the livers. Spread the blanched livers on a sheet pan. Let the water return to a boil and blanch the remaining chicken livers. Add them to the sheet pan. Refrigerate for at least 2 hours, or until completely cool.

3. In a large sauté pan, heat 2 tablespoons of the Clarified Butter over low heat. Add the shallots, garlic, and chopped thyme and sauté for 6 to 8 minutes, or until the shallots and garlic are tender.

4. Raise the heat to medium-high, add the Port, and cook for 3 to 4 minutes, or until most of the moisture evaporates. Remove from the heat and cool. Put the pan in the refrigerator and chill for at least 2 hours, or until completely cool.

5. In the bowl of a large food processor fitted with a metal blade, process the livers with the shallot mixture for about 2 minutes until blended and stiff. Add the butter and allspice and season to taste with salt and pepper. Process for 2 minutes longer, or until smooth and blended.

6. Line a $9 \times 5 \times 3$-inch terrine mold with plastic wrap, leaving 3-inch overhangs on the long sides of the terrine. Using a rubber spatula, spread the pâté in the terrine. Tap the mold on the countertop to remove any air pockets. Lay the whole thyme sprigs on top of the pâté. Pour the rest of the Clarified Butter over the top of the terrine and fold the overhanging ends of the plastic wrap over the top to cover. Smooth the plastic and refrigerate overnight or for at least 8 hours.

7. Before serving, preheat the broiler. Arrange the baguette slices on the broiler tray and broil about 2 inches from the heat for 30 to 45 seconds per side, or until brown.

8. To serve, use the overhanging plastic wrap to lift the pâté from the mold. Unwrap and cut the pâté into thin slices, then cut each slice in half on an angle. Arrange the two halves of the slice on a plate. Garnish each plate with 1 tablespoon of mustard, five cornichons, and a sprig of watercress. Serve with the toasted baguette slices.

MUSHROOM CAPS WITH DEVILED CRAB

For a cocktail party, it's always good to serve finger food that can be held and eaten with one hand. These fill the bill perfectly, plus they can be partially prepared well before serving.

Look for "stuffing mushrooms" in the supermarket—one 14-ounce package works well here. While we specify lump crabmeat, claw meat works very well, too. Just be sure it's free of any bits of shell for these elegant bites, and handle the crabmeat gently.

SERVES 6

12 medium white mushrooms, each 1½ to 2 inches wide, stemmed
2 teaspoons olive oil
Freshly ground white pepper
5 ounces lump crabmeat
3 tablespoons mayonnaise
2 teaspoons minced fresh curly-leaf parsley
2 teaspoons dry white wine
1 teaspoon dried tarragon
½ teaspoon English dry mustard
½ teaspoon Tabasco or other hot pepper sauce
Salt

1. Preheat the oven to 350°F.

2. Put the mushrooms, stem side up, on a wire rack. Place the rack on a baking sheet. Drizzle the oil over the mushrooms and season with white pepper to taste. Bake for 10 to 12 minutes, or until the caps are filled with liquid and they yield to the touch, but are still firm.

3. Remove the mushrooms from the oven and set aside at room temperature for a few minutes to cool slightly, upturned so that the liquid can drain. Remove the mushrooms from the rack, pat dry with paper towels, and transfer to the baking sheet. Refrigerate to cool.

4. Meanwhile, place the crabmeat in a medium mixing bowl and pick through to remove any bits of shell. Gently break the lumps apart.

5. Raise the oven temperature to 450°F.

6. In a small bowl, mix the mayonnaise, parsley, wine, tarragon, mustard, and Tabasco sauce. Season to taste with salt and pepper. Add to the crabmeat and toss to mix well.

7. Remove the baking sheet with the mushrooms from the refrigerator. Fill each mushroom cap with crab mixture and bake for about 10 minutes, or until golden brown. Allow to cool for a few minutes and serve warm.

BAKED CRAB CAKES WITH MUSTARD-MAYONNAISE SAUCE

I developed these crab cakes with John Bettin, the former president of Morton's, one weekend in my Chicago kitchen. Anytime you develop a recipe, you look at similar recipes and then use your own culinary wisdom and creativity—and we were thrilled with these results. Be sure to handle the crabmeat with care, and once the cakes are formed, handle them even more gently, as you would a ripe peach.

SERVES 6

1 pound fresh lump crabmeat (about 3 cups loosely packed)
1 cup Alex's Bread Crumbs (page 232)
1 large egg
8 tablespoons Mustard-Mayonnaise Sauce (page 222)
1 tablespoon chopped fresh curly-leaf parsley
1 teaspoon Dijon mustard
$\frac{1}{2}$ teaspoon Worcestershire sauce
$\frac{1}{4}$ teaspoon Tabasco sauce
6 tablespoons Clarified Butter (page 231), **melted, or olive oil**

1. Preheat the oven to 450°F.

2. Drain the crabmeat and put in a medium bowl. Pick through the crabmeat to remove any bits of shell, if necessary. Add the bread crumbs and gently toss until combined.

3. In a small bowl, whisk together the egg, 2 tablespoons of the Mustard-Mayonnaise Sauce, the parsley, mustard, and Worcestershire and Tabasco sauces. Pour this mixture over the crabmeat. Using a rubber spatula, gently fold the egg mixture into the crabmeat.

4. Divide the crabmeat into six equal portions, each measuring $1/2$ cup. Gently form each portion of crabmeat into a ball and flatten into a 1-inch-thick cake.

5. Put the butter in a 7×11-inch ovenproof dish and then put the crab cakes in the pan. Bake for 7 to 8 minutes, or until golden brown on the bottom. Gently turn the crab cakes and bake for 7 to 8 minutes longer, or until the cakes are golden brown on both sides and cooked through. Serve with the remaining 6 tablespoons of Mustard-Mayonnaise Sauce on the side.

GRILLED ASPARAGUS WITH ROASTED RED PEPPER

This is a nice, fresh alternative to meat and fish, and is a lovely combination of flavors. We use jumbo asparagus to go with our "bigger is better" theme, but you may use smaller stalks (either because that's all you can find or because you like them better). To peel the asparagus with a vegetable peeler, lay it on the countertop and peel in one direction so that the stalks don't break.

SERVES 6

2 large, thick-fleshed red bell peppers
36 thick asparagus spears (about 1½ pounds),
   all as close to the same size as possible
½ cup plus 2 tablespoons extra-virgin olive oil
¼ cup balsamic vinegar
1 tablespoon salt
1 tablespoon freshly ground white pepper
6 tablespoons balsamic glaze (see Note)
   or a balsamic-based vinaigrette

1. Char the peppers over a grill or a gas flame or under a broiler, until lightly blackened on all sides and barely softened. Put the peppers in a plastic bag and let rest at room temperature for about 5 minutes, or until cool enough to handle. Peel the skin off the peppers, but do not do this by running under water, which will wash away the flavorful oils.

2. Cut the peppers lengthwise through one side. Discard the ribs and seeds. Cut each pepper into three pieces. Set aside.

3. Break the tough, woody stems off of the asparagus, and then peel the bottom 2 inches of the stems to the white. The asparagus stems will break naturally where they should when bent.

4. Bring a large pot of salted water to a boil. Blanch the asparagus for 1 to 2 minutes, or until their color brightens. (Do not let the asparagus spears turn soft.) Drain and immediately submerge in cold water. Drain again. Dry with paper towels.

5. Preheat the broiler.

6. In a small bowl, whisk together $\frac{1}{2}$ cup of the oil with the vinegar, salt, and pepper. Transfer the asparagus to a baking sheet. Drizzle with the dressing and toss to coat.

7. Broil the asparagus, turning twice, for about 6 minutes, or until tender, rotating with tongs several times during cooking. Lightly brush the peppers with the remaining 2 tablespoons of oil.

8. Using a preheated countertop grill or a gas or charcoal grill, grill the peppers for about 1 minute, or until they have grill marks.

9. Center 2 pieces of pepper, grill sides up, on a plate. Fan six asparagus spears over the peppers. Repeat to make five more servings. Drizzle each with 1 tablespoon of balsamic glaze and serve immediately.

Note: Roland Balsamic Glaze is available in supermarkets. It's a concentrated sauce made with balsamic vinegar. We use it in the restaurant, but you may choose to use your favorite balsamic vinegar (aged is best) or favorite balsamic-based vinaigrette instead.

4

SALADS AND SOUPS

Morton's Caesar Salad

Chopped Salad with Hearts of Palm, Artichoke Hearts, and Blue Cheese

Summertime Tomato-Onion Salad

Spinach and Avocado Salad

Salad Niçoise with Pan-Seared Tuna

Morton's Salad with Blue Cheese Dressing

German Potato Soup

New England Clam Chowder

Black Bean Soup

Velvet Lobster Bisque

MORTON'S CAESAR SALAD

Without question, this is our most popular salad. In the old days, we made it tableside with old-fashioned flourish. It's now assembled in the kitchen but still has all the necessary ingredients for a great Caesar: crisp romaine, garlic, anchovies, and freshly grated Parmesan. No Caesar can be considered great without good croutons. Buy the best firm white bread you can. An unsliced Pullman loaf is ideal, but if you can't find one, thick-sliced sandwich bread works very well.

SERVES 6

2 slices firm, thick-sliced white bread, crusts removed
2 tablespoons Clarified Butter (page 231)**, melted, or olive oil**
3 tablespoons grated Parmesan cheese
1 teaspoon garlic powder
2 large heads romaine lettuce, each weighing a generous 1 pound,
   washed and dried
1 cup plus 2 tablespoons Caesar Dressing (page 229)

1. Preheat the oven to 375°F.

2. Cut each slice of bread into 16 to 20 cubes. Put the bread cubes in a bowl, drizzle with the butter, and toss to evenly coat. Spread the cubes in a single layer in a shallow baking pan. Bake for about 10 minutes, or until the croutons are golden brown. Shake the pan once or twice to encourage even browning.

3. Transfer the croutons to a medium mixing bowl. Sprinkle 1 tablespoon of the Parmesan and the garlic powder over the croutons. Gently toss. Set aside at room temperature.

4. Cut the lettuce into large bite-size pieces and transfer to a large salad or mixing bowl. Toss with the Caesar Dressing. Sprinkle the remaining Parmesan over the salad and add the croutons.

CHOPPED SALAD WITH HEARTS OF PALM, ARTICHOKE HEARTS, AND BLUE CHEESE

We have a faithful contingent who never fail to order this salad when they come to Morton's. Because the servings are so large, they sometimes split a salad—and if not, the salad can be a meal in itself. Use your favorite blue cheese and crisp lettuces, and when it comes to the tomatoes, be sure they are as fresh and ripe as you can find. If tomatoes aren't in season, omit them.

SERVES 6 TO 8

1 medium head iceberg lettuce, washed and dried
1 medium head romaine lettuce, washed and dried
10 to 12 frozen or canned (in brine) **artichoke hearts** (not marinated; about 12 ounces drained)
1 cup hearts of palm (about 12 ounces drained)
1 avocado
6 ounces blue cheese, such as Saga, Maytag, or gorgonzola, crumbled (1 cup)
¾ cup bacon bits, or 12 to 14 crumbled, crisp-cooked bacon strips
¾ cup chopped hard-cooked eggs (2 large eggs; see Note)
¾ cup finely minced red onion
¾ cup seeded, chopped plum tomato
¾ cup Dijon Vinaigrette (page 227)

1. Cut the iceberg and romaine lettuces into ½-inch squares. Transfer to a large mixing bowl. Cut the artichoke hearts into eighths and the hearts of palm into ¼-inch-long pieces and add to the lettuce.

2. Peel the avocado and remove the pit. Cut the avocado into ½-inch cubes and add to the lettuce.

3. Crumble the blue cheese over the salad. Sprinkle the bacon bits, chopped egg, onion, and tomato over the salad. Add the vinaigrette, toss well, and serve.

Note: To hard-cook eggs, put them in a saucepan with cold water to cover. Bring to a boil over medium-high heat. Cover, remove from the heat, and set aside for 15 minutes, during which time the eggs will harden. This is a better method than cooking the eggs in boiling water. There is less chance of the eggs cracking.

SUMMERTIME TOMATO-ONION SALAD

Make this salad only when tomatoes are in season. Nothing compares to a garden-fresh, vine-ripened tomato. During the late summer in Chicago, when I can get big, beautiful tomatoes from farmers' markets and friends' gardens, I make this salad all the time. You will, too.

SERVES 6

6 large, ripe tomatoes
6 leaves romaine lettuce
$\frac{1}{2}$ cup red wine vinegar
$1\frac{1}{2}$ teaspoons sugar
2 teaspoons dried oregano
1 cup flavorless vegetable oil, such as canola or safflower
Salt and freshly ground black pepper
2 tablespoons finely chopped ($\frac{1}{4}$-inch dice) red onion

1. Core the tomatoes, slice off the ends, and cut into thin slices, each about $\frac{1}{2}$ inch wide. Arrange the romaine leaves on a large platter and lay the tomato slices on top of the lettuce.

2. In a small bowl, whisk together the vinegar, sugar, and oregano. Slowly whisk in the oil until the dressing is mixed. Season to taste with salt and pepper. Drizzle over the tomatoes, using only as much as needed. (Reserve leftover dressing for another use.) Garnish the salad with chopped onion, season to taste with salt and pepper, and serve.

SPINACH AND AVOCADO SALAD

This salad is fresh and clean tasting, with the white wine vinegar and flavorless vegetable oil producing a light dressing that offsets the spinach perfectly, and the crumbled bacon and avocado lending it richness. Don't prepare the avocado until just before serving or the flesh will turn brown. The servings here are large enough to make a light lunch—or to serve more than six. Your choice.

SERVES 6

18 ounces fresh spinach leaves (not baby spinach)**, washed and dried**
2 to 3 strips bacon, or 2 generous tablespoons bacon bits
$2/3$ **cup white wine vinegar**
3 tablespoons sugar
$2^{1}/_{2}$ **teaspoons sweet paprika**
$1^{1}/_{4}$ **teaspoons Dijon mustard**
$1/4$ **teaspoon garlic powder**
$3/4$ **cup flavorless vegetable oil, such as canola or safflower**
12 fresh white mushrooms, stemmed and thinly sliced (about 3 cups)
3 avocados

1. Remove the thick spinach ribs and tear the leaves into bite-size pieces. Transfer to a large salad bowl.

2. In a small skillet or sauté pan, cook the bacon over medium heat for 5 to 6 minutes, or until crisp. Drain on paper towels, let cool, and then crumble.

3. In a small bowl, whisk together the vinegar, sugar, paprika, mustard, and garlic powder until the sugar is dissolved. Slowly whisk in the oil until mixed, to yield about $1^{1}/_{3}$ cups of dressing.

4. Pour the dressing over the spinach, add the mushrooms, and gently toss until thoroughly mixed.

5. Remove the skin and pits from the avocados. Cut the avocado flesh into $1/2$-inch cubes and add them to the salad. Toss very gently. Sprinkle the crumbled bacon over the salad and serve.

SALAD NIÇOISE WITH PAN-SEARED TUNA

The term **Niçoise** refers to any dish from the region around Nice, France, which includes the very Mediterranean ingredients of tomatoes, salty black olives, fresh herbs, and anchovies. The famous salad also includes green beans, potatoes, hard-cooked eggs, and tuna—very often canned tuna. We top the classic salad with pan-seared fresh tuna, which makes all the difference. This could easily be a full meal when you are in the mood for something light and refreshing. You could also serve it as a first course.

SERVES 6

2¼ pounds red potatoes (about 12 small-to-medium potatoes)
1½ pounds French green beans (haricots verts), **trimmed and halved if long**
6 large hard-cooked eggs (see Note, page 78)
1½ pounds fresh tuna, cut into six 4-ounce pieces
Salt and freshly ground black pepper
¼ cup Clarified Butter (page 231)
2¼ cups diced tomatoes (about 1 pound; 4 to 5 plum tomatoes)
1 cup chopped red onion
¾ cup pitted Niçoise olives (3 ounces drained weight)
18 anchovies, rinsed, patted dry, and finely chopped
1 cup plus 2 tablespoons Dijon Vinaigrette (page 227)
30 fresh chives
Six ¹⁄₁₆-inch-thick lemon slices

1. Bring a large pot of salted water to a boil. Add the potatoes, cover, and cook for about 20 minutes, or until tender. Drain. Spread the potatoes on a sheet pan and refrigerate until cool. Cut each cooled potato into five slices and set aside.

2. Bring a large pot of salted water to a boil. Blanch the green beans for 4 to 5 minutes, or until just tender. Drain and immediately submerge in cold water. Drain again and set aside.

3. Cut the eggs lengthwise into quarters and then cut across the quarters into ¼-inch-thick slices. Set aside.

4. Season the tuna with salt and pepper to taste. In a large sauté pan over medium-high heat, heat the butter until hot. Add the tuna and cook for about 1 minute on each side, or until seared and very lightly browned. If you prefer the tuna cooked a little more thoroughly, cook it for 1½ to 2 minutes on each side.

5. In a large mixing bowl, combine the potatoes, green beans, eggs, tomatoes, onion, olives, and anchovies. Gently toss with ¾ cup of the vinaigrette. Divide the salad among six large bowls.

6. Slice each piece of tuna into five thin slices and arrange the slices on top of the salad. Drizzle 1 tablespoon of the vinaigrette over the tuna in each bowl. Garnish each serving with five chives and a lemon slice.

MORTON'S SALAD WITH BLUE CHEESE DRESSING

As you can see, there is nothing to this salad other than the dressing. Begin with the best lettuces you can find and crown them with our famous blue cheese dressing. This salad was served at a restaurant owned by Arnie Morton's parents when he was a boy growing up in Chicago. One taste and you will understand why it has survived all these years and has now become one of our signature recipes.

SERVES 6 TO 8

1 large, heavy head iceberg lettuce (24 to 30 ounces), **washed and dried**
1 large head romaine lettuce (16 to 18 ounces), **washed and dried**
1½ cups Morton's Blue Cheese Dressing (page 228)

1. Tear the lettuce leaves into bite-size pieces and transfer to a large mixing bowl.

2. Toss with the dressing, and divide among six or eight plates.

CELEBRITY CLIP

Whenever Liza Minnelli is in Chicago she tries to come to Morton's to eat and signs autographs with good humor. On several occasions, her performance schedule has prevented her from dining at the steakhouse, so she calls in her order and we deliver it to her hotel room.

GERMAN POTATO SOUP

This was a staple in my mother's kitchen in the fall and winter, whether she was cooking in our restaurant or in our apartment above the restaurant. For me it's a taste of home. When you glance at the ingredients, it's no surprise it was cooked in so many households when I was growing up in Germany: everything is easy to come by and nothing is expensive. Plus, you can make it ahead of time because it holds wonderfully.

SERVES 6

3 slices smoked bacon
2 tablespoons flavorless vegetable oil, such as canola or safflower
1 cup finely chopped white onion (about $1/2$ large onion)
1 cup finely chopped celery (about 2 medium ribs)
1 cup finely chopped carrots (about 2 medium carrots)
$1/2$ cup finely chopped leek, white part only (about 1 medium leek)
$1^1/2$ quarts chicken broth
1 teaspoon dried marjoram
2 bay leaves
2 to 3 medium all-purpose or boiling potatoes (about 1 pound), **peeled and cut into $1/4$-inch cubes**
   (about 3 cups)
Salt and freshly ground black pepper
1 tablespoon chopped fresh flat-leaf parsley, for garnish

1. Chop the bacon into $1/4$-inch pieces. In a skillet, cook the bacon over medium heat for 5 to 6 minutes, or until browned and crisp. Remove with a slotted spoon, drain on paper towels, and set aside.

2. In a large pot, heat the oil over medium-high heat. Sauté the onion, celery, carrots, and leek for 4 to 5 minutes, until the vegetables soften without coloring.

3. Add the broth, marjoram, and bay leaves and bring to a boil. Add the potatoes and return to a boil. Reduce the heat to medium and simmer gently, partially covered, for about 20 minutes, or until the potatoes are soft. Discard the bay leaves. Season the soup with salt and pepper to taste.

4. Stir the bacon into the soup. Ladle into bowls and garnish with the chopped parsley.

NEW ENGLAND CLAM CHOWDER

New England clam chowder—the creamy kind—needs to be chock-full of clams. This is easy to make, especially if you use canned clams and bottled clam juice. For a chunkier, more robust soup, add more potatoes. But if you're serving it as a first course, as we do, there's no need. (See photograph on page 74.)

SERVES 6

26 ounces canned chopped clams (four 6½-ounce cans)
12 cups (3 quarts) **bottled clam juice** (twelve 8-ounce bottles)
4 cups half-and-half
¾ **teaspoon chicken base** (see Note, page 173) **or granulated bouillon** (optional)
5 tablespoons unsalted butter
½ **cup finely diced celery**
¼ **cup finely diced Spanish onion**
1½ **cups finely diced potato**
1¼ **cups finely diced leek**
½ **bay leaf**
½ **teaspoon dried thyme**
Salt and freshly ground white pepper
⅓ **cup plus 2 tablespoons all-purpose flour**
Dash of Tabasco sauce
¼ **cup dry sherry**
2 tablespoons chopped fresh curly-leaf parsley, for garnish

1. Drain the chopped clams and reserve the liquid. Set aside the clams.

2. In a large stockpot, combine the liquid from the chopped clams and the clam juice and bring to a boil over medium-high heat. Reduce the heat to medium and simmer, uncovered, for 35 to 45 minutes, or until the clam juice is reduced by half.

3. Add the half-and-half and chicken base, if using. Bring the liquid to a boil, reduce the heat to medium, and simmer for 2 to 3 minutes. Set aside.

4. In another large stockpot, melt 4 tablespoons of the butter over medium heat. Add the celery, onion, potato, leek, bay leaf, and thyme, and season to taste with salt and pepper. Sauté the vegetables for 3 to 4 minutes, or until softened. Sprinkle the flour over the vegetables and cook, stirring constantly, for 3 to 5 minutes, until the flour and vegetables are well integrated. The mixture will be stiff at first.

5. Add the reserved liquid and bring to a boil over medium-high heat, stirring frequently until thickened and smooth. Add the remaining 1 tablespoon of butter, the reserved clams, and the Tabasco sauce and cook, stirring gently, just until the butter is incorporated. Remove from the heat and stir in the sherry. Ladle the soup into six soup bowls and garnish each serving with chopped parsley.

BLACK BEAN SOUP

I am truly fond of this hearty soup. Periodically we take it off the menu to make room for another soup, but we always end up reinstating it. It's never off the menu in my home kitchen, nor should it be in yours. I do think it tastes best if you soak your own beans, although if you wanted to substitute canned black beans, you certainly could. This can be a meal on its own, served with a salad and good bread.

SERVES 6

1 pound dried black beans
2 slices bacon, diced (¼ cup)
1 small to medium Spanish onion, diced (¾ cup)
2 medium carrots, peeled and diced (¾ cup)
1 small celery rib, diced (¼ cup)
1½ teaspoons minced garlic
8 cups canned chicken broth
2¼ teaspoons chili powder
1¼ teaspoons ground cumin
¾ teaspoon freshly ground white pepper, plus more to taste
Salt
4 tablespoons diced red onion or green onion, for garnish
½ cup sour cream, for garnish

1. Rinse the beans and transfer to a bowl. Cover the beans with cold water and let soak for at least 8 hours or overnight. Drain and change the water two or three times during soaking, if possible.

2. In a large stockpot, cook the bacon over medium-low heat for about 5 minutes, or until the fat is rendered and the bacon is starting to crisp. Add the onion, carrots, celery, and garlic and cook, partially covered, for 8 to 10 minutes, or until the vegetables are tender. Drain the beans and add them to the pot. Add the chicken broth, chili powder, cumin, and pepper.

3. Raise the heat to high and bring the liquid to a boil. Reduce the heat to medium and simmer, partially covered, stirring occasionally, for about $1^{1}/_{2}$ hours, or until the beans are soft but still hold their shape. Season to taste with salt.

4. Using a handheld immersion blender, purée the soup until smooth. Thin with more chicken broth or water, if necessary. Season to taste with salt and pepper. (Alternatively, blend the soup, in batches, in a blender.) To serve, divide the soup among six bowls. Serve with diced onion and dollops of sour cream.

CELEBRITY CLIP

The staff of our Beverly Hills restaurant is always thrilled when Brad Garrett, who plays Robert, Ray Romano's brother on television's **Everybody Loves Raymond,** calls to reserve the boardroom for a private party. This is a fairly common occurrence. Brad and his buddies stay until the wee hours, and everyone, including the staff, has a great time. And guess what? Brad is even funnier in person! Recently he called to let us know he was going to be in New York playing the role of Murray the Cop in **The Odd Couple** on Broadway starring Matthew Broderick and Nathan Lane. Guess now our New York Morton's will have all the fun!

VELVET LOBSTER BISQUE

This is a very elegant dish—smooth, rich, and gloriously seductive. It's one of the few recipes in the book that require some advance planning and even a little fuss. Making the lobster stock takes time, and you need to buy lobsters for their shells (which is expensive), and then find something else to do with the lobster meat (which in my opinion is not a terrible hardship!). You will also need two large stockpots. While there are no shortcuts, either for us in our restaurant kitchens or for you in your home kitchen, try this at least once for a special occasion. It's sublimely delicious.

SERVES 10; MAKES ABOUT 3 QUARTS

2 quarts Lobster Bisque Stock (recipe follows)
4 cups heavy cream
1 cup dry white wine
½ packed cup cornstarch
1 tablespoon brandy
1½ teaspoons salt
½ teaspoon freshly ground white pepper
¼ teaspoon cayenne pepper
Lobster meat from stock, warmed (see Note), **for garnish**
Chopped fresh curly-leaf parsley, for garnish

1. In a large pot, bring the Lobster Bisque Stock to a boil over medium-high heat. Stir in the heavy cream.

2. In a small bowl, whisk together the wine and cornstarch until smooth. Add to the hot stock and whisk constantly for 3 to 4 minutes, or until the soup simmers and thickens.

3. Stir in the brandy, salt, white pepper, and cayenne. Serve immediately, garnished with lobster meat and parsley.

Note: To warm the lobster meat, bring a medium saucepan of water to a boil. Remove the pan from the heat, drop the lobster meat into the hot water for 45 seconds, and then drain well.

LOBSTER BISQUE STOCK

MAKES 2 QUARTS

3½ to 4 pounds small (chicken) lobsters or other fresh lobsters (see Note)
1½ tablespoons extra-virgin olive oil
2 medium carrots, peeled and roughly chopped (about ¾ cup)
1 medium Spanish onion, roughly chopped (about ¾ cup)
1 large celery rib, roughly chopped (about ¾ cup)
1 garlic clove, chopped
⅔ cup tomato paste
8 curly-leaf parsley sprigs, rinsed well and thick stems trimmed

1. In a large stockpot, bring about 5 gallons of water to a rolling boil over high heat. Add the lobsters and cook, partially covered, at a gentle boil for 15 to 18 minutes, or until the lobsters are red. Remove the lobsters with tongs, drain in a colander, reserving the lobster cooking water, and set aside for at least 30 minutes to cool.

2. When the lobsters are cool enough to handle, remove the meat from the lobsters, including the claws and tails, reserving the shells. Cut the meat into large chunks, trimming any rough edges, and reserve the meat, covered in the refrigerator, to garnish the bisque.

3. Put the remaining lobster shells in two heavy-duty plastic bags. Wrap the bags in a kitchen towel and smash the shells with a mallet, a rolling pin, or the flat side of a skillet.

4. Meanwhile, in another large stockpot, heat the oil over medium heat. When the oil is hot, add the carrots, onion, celery, and garlic and sauté, partially covered, for about 10 minutes, or until the vegeta-bles are tender and lightly browned. Add the crushed lobster shells and sauté for about 15 minutes.

5. Add 12 cups of the reserved lobster cooking water and bring to a boil over high heat. Add the tomato paste and parsley and stir well. Reduce the heat to medium and simmer the stock, partially covered, for 1½ hours, skimming off any fat and froth that float to the surface of the liquid.

6. Strain the stock through a chinois or a fine-mesh sieve into a large metal bowl, pressing down on the vegetables and shells to release all the liquid. You need 8 cups of liquid. If necessary, pour additional lobster cooking water or tap water over the shells in the sieve and into the bowl until you have 8 cups. Discard the shells and vegetables.

7. If not using right away, put the bowl in a larger bowl of ice and water and let cool. Cover and refrigerate for several hours, or until chilled. Transfer the stock to a covered storage container and refrigerate for up to 4 days. The stock can be frozen for up to 7 days if frozen as soon as it's prepared.

NOTE: Small lobsters have thinner, softer shells than larger ones and so are easier to crush. They also may be less expensive than larger ones. You don't need to buy small lobsters, though. Larger lobsters will also work.

5

STEAK: OUR FEATURE PRESENTATION

Porterhouse Steak

New York Strip Steak

Filet Mignon

Beef Filet Diane

Cajun Ribeye Steak

Kansas City Bone-In Strip Steak

T-Bone Steak

Steak au Poivre

Beef Filet Oskar

MORTON'S TIPS FOR A PERFECT STEAK

In chapter 1, we discussed how to select steaks. In the recipe notes throughout the book, we offer more specific tips depending on the cut. Once you get the steak home, you'll want to cook it to perfection—just as we do at the steakhouse.

First, I can't emphasize enough how important it is that the meat be at room temperature before you cook it. In each recipe we say to leave it out for 30 to 60 minutes before cooking. This does not apply to chopped meat, which should be kept refrigerated until shortly before cooking, nor do we suggest you ever leave meat on the countertop for any longer than an hour. If the day is very hot or if your kitchen feels tropical, 30 minutes should be ample.

Once the chill is off the meat, we season it lightly but evenly with seasoned salt. At Morton's, we have our own blend, made for us by a supplier. This is not available to the public, so rely on your favorite seasoned salt (such as Lawry's).

During cooking, the naturally occurring fat in the steak, called marbling, softens and much of it melts. The fatty acids release pleasing aromatic compounds as well as wonderful flavor compounds that are only found in beef. This is one reason why a well-marbled steak will give you better flavor than one that is too lean. Marbling also ensures juiciness.

When a steak is on the grill or under the broiler, turn it only once. Use tongs so that the meat is never punctured. Test steak doneness by feel. You may have seen chefs pressing their fingers into meat on the grill. To understand what they are doing, hold your hand out, palm up, and follow these guidelines:

FOR EXTRA-RARE AND RARE MEAT
Poke the pad at the base of the thumb. If the meat feels like this, it's ready.
The softer the meat, the rarer.

FOR MEDIUM-RARE MEAT
Press the area of your palm between the thumb pad and the center of the palm.
If the meat feels like this, it's ready.

FOR MEDIUM MEAT
Press the middle of your palm. If the meat feels like this, it's ready.

FOR WELL-DONE MEAT
Press the base of the pinkie. If the meat feels like this, it's ready.

This is not a foolproof method, but it's a good place to start. Different cuts of meat will feel different from one another, but the **degree** of difference between rare and medium-rare, and so on, will be the same. For instance, a medium-rare porterhouse will feel firmer than a medium-rare tenderloin, and these two cuts also feel quite different when raw.

There are other tests for doneness. For example, if you're cooking a steak with a bone, such as a porterhouse or T-bone, the steak is medium-rare when the meat is still firmly attached to the bone. When it starts to pull away from the bone, it's past medium-rare and on its way to medium.

We never recommend poking holes in meat as it cooks; too many valuable juices can escape. But if you are more comfortable using an instant-read thermometer, do so, particularly when you are learning how to determine when the steak is done by feel. (For the correct internal temperatures, turn to page 18.) It won't be long before you no longer need to puncture the meat but will know just by feel when it's perfectly cooked.

PORTERHOUSE STEAK

I think porterhouse is a great favorite because of its generous piece of filet. The steak is cut from the short loin near the sirloin, and the steaks we serve are between $1\frac{1}{4}$ and $1\frac{1}{2}$ inches thick (although it may be difficult for you to find such thick steaks). How the steak got its name is not well documented, but it most likely comes from another term for an old-fashioned coach stop, or porter house, where weary travelers could enjoy a good steak and draft of ale.

When you buy porterhouse steaks, ask for the center cut, which has the biggest filet, and look for moderately abundant marbling and a tail that tapers to a width of $\frac{1}{2}$ inch or less. When the meat reaches the ideal medium-rare, it will visibly tighten along the bone as it begins to pull away from it.

WINE RECOMMENDATION: Cabernet Sauvignon or Sangiovese

SERVES 6

Three 24-ounce aged porterhouse steaks,
each about $1\frac{1}{2}$ inches thick
Vegetable oil cooking spray
2 tablespoons seasoned salt
6 tablespoons Au Jus (optional; page 210)

1. Remove the steaks from the refrigerator and let them rest at room temperature for 30 to 60 minutes.

2. Prepare a charcoal or gas grill or preheat the broiler and position a rack 4 inches from the heating element. Lightly spray the grill rack with vegetable oil cooking spray. The coals should be medium-hot for the charcoal grill. The burners should be on high for the gas grill.

3. Season the steaks lightly on both sides with the seasoned salt. If using a charcoal grill, grill for 6 to 8 minutes. Turn, using tongs, and grill the other side for 6 to 8 minutes for medium-rare, or until the desired degree of doneness. If using a gas grill, grill for 6 to 8 minutes. Turn, using tongs, and grill the other side for 5 to 6 minutes for medium-rare, or until the desired degree of doneness. For medium-well, grill for 10 minutes on the first side and for 5 minutes on the second side. If using the broiler, broil 4 inches from the heat source for 8 to 10 minutes. Turn, using tongs, and broil the other side for 6 to 8 minutes for medium-rare, or until the desired degree of doneness.

4. To serve, slice the steaks and spoon some of the Au Jus on top, if desired.

NEW YORK STRIP STEAK

This steak is also known as a New York sirloin or a New York steak, or just a sirloin, and as a rule it is a large piece of meat. Like other tender steaks, this is cut from the short loin. When you buy it, be sure it's a nice rosy red with a good sprinkling of fat and has ¼ inch of cap fat—that is, the outside rim of the steak should be topped with creamy-looking fat. Avoid strip steaks with an obvious vein running through the meat; this vein tightens during cooking so that the meat folds in on itself.

WINE RECOMMENDATION: Cabernet Sauvignon or Red Bordeaux

SERVES 6

> **Three 20-ounce aged New York strip steaks,**
> **each about 2 inches thick**
> **Vegetable oil cooking spray**
> **1 tablespoon seasoned salt**
> **6 tablespoons Au Jus** (optional; page 210)

1. Remove the steaks from the refrigerator and let them rest at room temperature for 30 to 60 minutes.

2. Prepare a charcoal or gas grill or preheat the broiler and position a rack 4 inches from the heating element. Lightly spray the grill rack with vegetable oil cooking spray. The coals should be medium-hot for the charcoal grill. The burners should be on high for the gas grill.

3. Season the steaks lightly on both sides with the seasoned salt. If using a charcoal grill, grill for 10 minutes. Turn, using tongs, and grill the other side for 9 to 11 minutes for medium-rare, or until the desired degree of doneness. If using a gas grill, grill for 10 minutes. Turn, using tongs, and grill the other side for 9 to 10 minutes for medium-rare, or until the desired degree of doneness. If using the broiler, broil 4 inches from the heat source for 10 minutes. Turn, using tongs, and broil the other side for 10 to 11 minutes for medium-rare, or until the desired degree of doneness.

4. To serve, slice the steaks and spoon some of the Au Jus on top, if desired.

FILET MIGNON

The leanest of the steaks, filet mignon is also the most popular at the restaurant as well as among home cooks. Cut from the bottom of the short loin, it's a steak sliced from the tenderloin and as such is tender as well as lean. It lacks the same robust beef flavor some of the other cuts have, but makes up for it with its buttery texture.

All fat and silver skin should be removed, which is how it's usually sold for the home cook (called a barrel cut). At Morton's we leave a little silver skin and about $1/8$ inch of fat on our filet mignon to protect the meat from the high temperatures of restaurant cooking. Don't overcook filet mignon. When perfectly grilled or broiled, it needs no fanfare. Filet mignon speaks for itself!

WINE RECOMMENDATION: Merlot or Pinot Noir

SERVES 6

Six 14-ounce filets mignons, each 2 to 2$1/2$ inches thick
Vegetable oil cooking spray
Seasoned salt
6 tablespoons Au Jus (optional; page 210)

1. Remove the steaks from the refrigerator and let them rest at room temperature for 30 to 60 minutes.

2. Prepare a charcoal or gas grill or preheat the broiler and position a rack 4 inches from the heating element. Lightly spray the grill rack with vegetable oil cooking spray. The coals should be medium-hot for the charcoal grill. The burners should be on high for the gas grill.

3. Season the steaks lightly on both sides with the seasoned salt. If using a charcoal grill, grill for about 8 minutes. Turn, using tongs, and grill the other side for 6 to 8 minutes for medium-rare, or until the desired degree of doneness. If using a gas grill, grill for about 8 minutes. Turn, using tongs, and grill the other side for 6 to 8 minutes for medium-rare, or until the desired degree of doneness. If using the broiler, broil 4 inches from the heat source for 9 minutes. Turn, using tongs, and broil the other side for 8 to 10 minutes for medium-rare, or until the desired degree of doneness.

4. To serve, spoon some of the Au Jus over the steaks, if desired.

BEEF FILET DIANE

If you are going to make a sauce for tender, delicately flavored filet mignon, I suggest this one. It's made with everything that goes best with steak: mushrooms, garlic, red wine, and cream. You can make the sauce ahead of time and keep it warm until the steaks are cooked. This is a lovely way to dress up steak for a dinner party or a special feast.

WINE RECOMMENDATION: Merlot or Pinot Noir

SERVES 6

Six ¾-inch-thick slices dense white bread
14 tablespoons unsalted butter
4 tablespoons finely chopped garlic
½ cup dry red wine
½ cup Cognac
3 cups reconstituted store-bought
   veal demi-glace (see Note, page 111)
2 teaspoons Dijon mustard
2 teaspoons Worcestershire sauce
2 teaspoons tomato paste
1⅓ cups heavy cream
20 ounces white or cremini mushrooms, stemmed and
   sliced about ¼ inch thick (about 6 cups)
Six 10-ounce filets mignons, each about
   2½ inches thick
Seasoned salt
Chopped fresh flat-leaf parsley, for garnish

recipe continues

CELEBRITY CLIP

When Michael Jordan was playing for the Chicago Bulls, he was a frequent guest at the restaurant but could never sign autographs because of a contractual agreement. One day a young boy who was eating at Morton's with his parents was so excited to see the famous basketball star, he could barely contain himself. Jordan relented and signed a random page of a magazine we had on hand and gave the boy the magazine. That was one excited kid!

1. Preheat the oven to 400°F.

2. Lay the bread slices on a work surface. Using a 3-inch-wide round cookie cutter or water glass, cut out six rounds. Transfer the rounds to a baking sheet. Bake, turning once, for 5 to 7 minutes, or until the croutons are light golden brown and crisp. Watch them carefully; they brown quickly around the edges. Cool on wire racks.

3. In a saucepan over medium heat, melt 2 tablespoons of the butter. Add the garlic and cook, stirring frequently, for 2 to 3 minutes, or until softened. Add the wine and Cognac. Raise the heat to medium-high and simmer, uncovered, for 8 to 10 minutes, or until most of the liquid has evaporated. Add the demi-glace, mustard, Worcestershire sauce, and tomato paste. Bring to a simmer over medium heat and add the cream. Return to a boil and reduce the sauce, whisking often, for about 15 minutes, or until the sauce thickens to a creamy consistency and deepens in color.

4. In a large sauté pan, melt the remaining 12 tablespoons of butter over medium-high heat. Add the mushrooms and sauté for about 5 minutes, or until the mushrooms begin to release their moisture and start to soften.

5. Stir the sauce into the mushrooms and heat over low heat until gently simmering. Let the sauce simmer over low heat for 12 to 15 minutes, until reduced to about 6 cups and slightly thickened. Cover and keep warm over very low heat until ready to serve.

6. Remove the steaks from the refrigerator and let them rest at room temperature for 30 to 60 minutes. Season them lightly on both sides with the seasoned salt.

7. Preheat the broiler if using an electric broiler.

8. Broil the steaks about 4 inches from the heat source for 5 to 6 minutes per side for rare, 6 to 7 minutes per side for medium-rare, or until the desired degree of doneness.

9. To serve, place a filet on top of each crouton. Ladle some of the sauce over the steaks. Garnish with chopped parsley. Pass the remaining sauce on the side.

CAJUN RIBEYE STEAK

Ribeye steaks are hugely popular with restaurant guests but are not always on the tip of the tongue when home cooks think of buying steak. This is a shame because this cut, from the prime rib section, is a rich-tasting steak. It is full of flavor and nearly as tender as a steak from the short loin, so you won't go wrong with a ribeye. It should be well marbled and may or may not have a noticeable nugget of creamy fat embedded in the meat. When a ribeye is sold with its bone, it's called a bone-in rib steak—and is delicious. You can use any Cajun seasoning rub for this steak or try our blend. Apply the rub generously, working it into the meat with your fingers before submerging it in oil to marinate overnight.

WINE RECOMMENDATION: Shiraz, Syrah, Red Zinfandel, or Rhone Valley Red

SERVES 6

> **1 cup plus 2 tablespoons Morton's Cajun Seasoning** (recipe follows) **or other Cajun seasoning**
> **Six 16-ounce aged ribeye steaks, each about 1½ inches thick**
> **4¾ cups flavorless vegetable oil, such as canola or safflower**
> **6 tablespoons Au Jus** (optional; page 210)

1. Put the Morton's Cajun Seasoning in a large, shallow glass or ceramic pan. Press each side of the steaks into the seasoning to cover completely. Remove the steaks and lightly pound each four to five times on both sides with a meat mallet or small, heavy skillet to soften but not flatten more than a little. Discard any remaining seasoning in the pan.

2. Pour the oil into the pan and add the steaks one by one. They should be covered with oil; add more if necessary. Cover with plastic wrap and refrigerate for at least 8 hours and up to 24 hours. Alternatively, marinate the steaks in heavy-duty resealable plastic bags.

3. When you are ready to cook the steaks, remove them from the oil and pat off excess oil with paper towels. The oil can flair on the grill or in the broiler. Set the steaks aside for 30 to 60 minutes at room temperature.

recipe continues

4. Prepare a charcoal or gas grill or preheat the broiler and position a rack 4 inches from the heating element. The coals should be medium-hot for the charcoal grill. The burners should be on high for the gas grill.

5. If using a charcoal grill, grill for about 8 minutes. Turn, using tongs, and grill the other side for 8 to 9 minutes for medium-rare, or until the desired degree of doneness. If using a gas grill, grill for about 8 minutes. Turn, using tongs, and grill the other side for 8 to 9 minutes for medium-rare, or until the desired degree of doneness. If using the broiler, broil 4 inches from the heat source for about 8 minutes. Turn, using tongs, and broil the other side for about 8 minutes for medium-rare, or until the desired degree of doneness.

6. To serve, spoon some of the Au Jus over the steaks, if desired.

MORTON'S CAJUN SEASONING
MAKES ABOUT 2½ CUPS

½ cup paprika
⅓ cup salt
⅓ cup freshly ground white pepper
⅓ cup garlic powder
⅓ cup onion powder
2½ tablespoons dried thyme (see Note)
2½ tablespoons dried oregano
2½ tablespoons freshly ground black pepper
2½ tablespoons cayenne pepper

1. In a mixing bowl, stir together all the ingredients.

2. When mixed, transfer to an airtight container and store in a cool dark place. The seasoning will keep for up to 3 months.

NOTE: You do not have to be perfectly precise when measuring these dried herbs. If you feel better with precision, 2½ tablespoons equals 2 tablespoons plus 1½ teaspoons.

KANSAS CITY BONE-IN STRIP STEAK

This bone-in steak is the porterhouse without the filet. It's called a Kansas City strip steak, named after the city that popularized the cut, but your butcher may call it shell steak. It's cut from the short loin once the tenderloin strip has been removed, and is one of the tastiest steaks we serve. This steak may be cut to thicknesses ranging from 1 to 2½ inches.

WINE RECOMMENDATION: Cabernet Sauvignon or Red Bordeaux

SERVES 6

**Six 18-ounce Kansas City bone-in strip steaks,
each about 2 inches thick
Vegetable oil cooking spray
Seasoned salt
6 tablespoons Au Jus** (optional; page 210)

1. Remove the steaks from the refrigerator and let them rest at room temperature for 30 to 60 minutes.

2. Prepare a charcoal or gas grill or preheat the broiler and position a rack 4 inches from the heating element. Lightly spray the grill rack with vegetable oil cooking spray. The coals should be medium-hot for the charcoal grill. The burners should be on high for the gas grill.

3. Season the steaks lightly on both sides with the seasoned salt. If using a charcoal grill, grill for 10 minutes. Turn, using tongs, and grill the other side for 10 to 12 minutes for medium-rare, or until the desired degree of doneness. If using a gas grill, grill for 9 minutes. Turn, using tongs, and grill the other side for 8 to 9 minutes for medium-rare, or until the desired degree of doneness. If using the broiler, broil 4 inches from the heat source for 12 minutes. Turn, using tongs, and broil the other side for 11 to 12 minutes for medium-rare, or until the desired degree of doneness.

4. To serve, spoon some of the Au Jus over the steaks, if desired.

T-BONE STEAK

The eye of the filet on a T-bone steak is smaller than the eye of the porterhouse, which only means it's cut further down the rib and has a smaller tail. It may also have a noticeable vein running through it, which can't be helped. Slice the vein three or four times with a sharp knife so that it won't tighten during cooking.

WINE RECOMMENDATION: Cabernet Sauvignon or Red Bordeaux

SERVES 6

Three 21-ounce T-bone steaks
Vegetable oil cooking spray
Seasoned salt
6 tablespoons Au Jus (optional; page 210)

1. Remove the steaks from the refrigerator and let them rest at room temperature for 30 to 60 minutes.

2. Prepare a charcoal or gas grill or preheat the broiler and position a rack 4 inches from the heating element. Lightly spray the grill rack with vegetable oil cooking spray. The coals should be medium-hot for the charcoal grill. The burners should be on high for the gas grill.

3. Season the steaks lightly on both sides with the seasoned salt. If using a charcoal grill, grill for 10 minutes. Turn, using tongs, and grill the other side for 10 to 12 minutes for medium-rare, or until the desired degree of doneness. If using a gas grill, grill for 10 minutes. Turn, using tongs, and grill the other side for 11 to 13 minutes for medium-rare, or until the desired degree of doneness. If using the broiler, broil 4 inches from the heat source for 8 minutes. Turn, using tongs, and broil the other side for 6 to 7 minutes for medium-rare, or until the desired degree of doneness.

4. To serve, slice the steaks and spoon some of the Au Jus on top, if desired.

STEAK AU POIVRE

Our steak au poivre is made a little differently from some versions of the classic. We don't press the peppercorns into the meat but rely entirely on the sauce for the peppery flavor. The creamy sauce is made with plenty of crushed peppercorns but without brandy, a common ingredient in the French version of the sauce. We suggest Kansas City bone-in steaks, also known as shell steaks. Our recipe for the Peppercorn Sauce makes more than you will need, but it's tricky to make much less than 2 cups. You can freeze the peppercorn base before the cream is added for future use.

WINE RECOMMENDATION: Shiraz, Syrah, Red Zinfandel, or Rhone Valley Red

SERVES 6

Three 18-ounce Kansas City bone-in steaks, about 2 inches thick
Vegetable oil cooking spray
Seasoned salt
2 cups Peppercorn Sauce (recipe follows)

1. Remove the steaks from the refrigerator and let them rest at room temperature for 30 to 60 minutes.

2. Prepare a charcoal or gas grill or preheat the broiler and position a rack 4 inches from the heating element. Lightly spray the grill rack with vegetable oil cooking spray. The coals should be medium-hot for the charcoal grill. The burners should be on high for the gas grill.

3. Season the steaks lightly on both sides with the seasoned salt. If using a charcoal grill, grill for 10 minutes. Turn, using tongs, and grill the other side for 10 to 12 minutes for medium-rare, or until the desired degree of doneness. If using a gas grill, grill for 10 minutes. Turn, using tongs, and grill the other side for 11 to 13 minutes for medium-rare, or until the desired degree of doneness. If using the broiler, broil

recipe continues

4 inches from the heat source for 12 minutes. Turn, using tongs, and broil the other side for 11 to 12 minutes for medium-rare, or until the desired degree of doneness.

4. Meanwhile, heat the Peppercorn Sauce, if it's not already warm.

5. To serve, slice the steaks and spoon some of the sauce on top. Serve any extra sauce on the side, if desired.

PEPPERCORN SAUCE
MAKES ABOUT 2 CUPS

1 tablespoon unsalted butter
$1\frac{1}{2}$ tablespoons chopped shallots
2 tablespoons cracked red, green, white, and black peppercorns (see Note)
$\frac{1}{2}$ cup Cognac
3 tablespoons undiluted store-bought veal demi-glace (see Note)
$\frac{3}{4}$ cup heavy cream
Salt

1. In a sauté pan, melt the butter over low heat. Add the shallots and peppercorns and sauté for about 5 minutes, or until the shallots soften. Add the Cognac, raise the heat to medium, and cook until the Cognac evaporates almost completely. Add $\frac{3}{4}$ cup of water and the demi-glace. Bring to a boil, stirring until the demi-glace dissolves. Add the cream and bring to a simmer. Cook for about 5 minutes, or until thickened. Season to taste with salt.

2. Set aside to cool. When cool, cover and refrigerate for up to 3 days.

NOTES: Peppercorn mixes are easy to find in supermarkets and specialty stores. If you have only black peppercorns, use them instead.

You can buy veal demi-glace in a small container, usually about $1\frac{1}{2}$ ounces, in specialty food stores, some supermarkets, and even some price clubs. We like More Than Gourmet Demi-Glace Gold. To find a convenient location or to order it online, go to http://www.morethangourmet.com.

BEEF FILET OSKAR

Without question, this is an indulgent way to serve steak. The filet steaks (filets mignons) are served with lump crabmeat and our very own Béarnaise Sauce. Look for large asparagus because they will best support the crab-meat and look great on top of the filet. Just as you look for the best meat, buy the best lump crabmeat you can. Everything for this very special dish must be first-rate!

WINE RECOMMENDATION: Pinot Noir or Red Burgundy

SERVES 6

Six 8- to 9-ounce filets mignons, each about 2 inches thick
Vegetable oil cooking spray
Seasoned salt
12 slices very thin white bread
12 large asparagus spears
12 ounces fresh lump crabmeat (2 loosely packed cups)
2¼ cups Béarnaise Sauce (page 214), **warmed**

1. Remove the steaks from the refrigerator and let them rest at room temperature for 30 to 60 minutes.

2. Preheat the oven to 400°F.

3. Prepare a charcoal or gas grill or preheat the broiler and position a rack 4 inches from the heating element. Lightly spray the grill rack with vegetable oil cooking spray. The coals should be medium-hot for the charcoal grill. The burners should be on high for the gas grill.

4. Season the filets lightly on both sides with the seasoned salt.

5. Lay the bread slices on a work surface. Using a 3-inch-wide round cookie cutter or water glass, cut out 12 rounds. Transfer the rounds to a baking sheet. Bake, turning once, for 5 to 7 minutes, or until the croutons are light golden brown and crisp. Watch them carefully; they brown quickly around the edges. Cool on wire racks.

6. Lower the oven temperature to 300°F.

7. In a large skillet filled about halfway with boiling water and set over medium-high heat, blanch the asparagus spears for 2 to 3 minutes, or until fork-tender. Cut each asparagus spear in half crosswise and then split each half lengthwise. Lay the split spears in a single layer around the perimeter of an 11×17-inch baking pan. Place the crabmeat in the center of the pan. Heat the asparagus and crabmeat in the oven for 8 to 10 minutes, or until heated through. Remove from the oven and cover to keep warm.

8. Meanwhile, if using a charcoal grill, grill the steaks for about 5 minutes. Turn, using tongs, and grill the other side for about 5 minutes for medium-rare, or until the desired degree of doneness. If using a gas grill, grill for about 5 minutes. Turn, using tongs, and grill the other side for about 5 minutes for medium-rare, or until the desired degree of doneness. If using the broiler, broil 4 inches from the heat source for 8 minutes. Turn, using tongs, and broil the other side for 7 to 8 minutes for medium-rare, or until the desired degree of doneness.

9. Cut each filet in half against the grain and put each portion, cut side up, on a crouton. Put two croutons on each serving plate. Put four asparagus pieces (two with tips) on top of each filet half to form a squared crosshatch (#) design. Divide the crab evenly among the plates, resting it on the asparagus. Spoon Béarnaise Sauce over each serving and pass any extra sauce on the side.

6

OTHER STEAKHOUSE FAVORITES

Morton's Prime Rib Roast

Chopped Steak

Morton's Hamburgers

Morton's Beef Wellington

Beef Rouladen

Chicago Pepper Steak

Beef Tenderloin Brochettes with
   Diablo Sauce

Romanian Skirt Steak with Golden
   Garlic and Fried Parsley

Lamb Chops with Baked Apples

Braised Lamb Shanks with Root
   Vegetables and Mashed Potatoes

Broiled Veal Chops

Klaus's Wiener Schnitzel

Sicilian Veal Chops

Chicken Christopher

Baked Lemon-Oregano Chicken

Broiled Lemon Chicken
   with Linguini

Baked Lobster with Cream

Shrimp Alexander with
   Beurre Blanc

Swordfish with Béarnaise Sauce

Salmon with Beurre Blanc

Baked Cod with Alex's Bread
   Crumbs

Florida Grouper with Tomatoes

Linguini with Clams and Shrimp

MORTON'S PRIME RIB ROAST

This is a very festive cut, perfect for a holiday dinner or a party. In this recipe, we give instructions for cooking a very large rib roast—one with all seven ribs, weighing a good 12 pounds—that is best suited for both a large oven and a large group. You might prefer to roast a smaller piece of meat; a three- to four-rib roast will easily serve five or six people. It's important to let the meat sit at room temperature for about 1 hour before roasting; if it's too cold when you put it in the oven, it won't cook evenly. In my opinion, a prime rib cooked any more than medium-rare might as well be pot roast. This is not true for the end pieces, which are many people's favorites because they are crisp and salty and have great flavor. (There's always someone at the table who claims the end piece!) Finally, when you roast a rib roast, the house fills with an aroma that can't be beat.

We cook our roasts on beds of rock salt, which heats up in the oven and holds the temperature for very even cooking. If you prefer to omit it, ensure even cooking by setting the roast on a rack so that it does not sit directly on the bottom of the pan.

WINE RECOMMENDATION: Shiraz, Syrah, Red Zinfandel, or Cabernet Sauvignon

SERVES 10 TO 12

One 12- to 14-pound seven-rib aged prime rib
½ cup seasoned salt
About 4½ pounds rock salt (see Note)
¾ cup Au Jus (optional; page 210)
1 to 1½ cups Whipped Horseradish (page 218)

1. A day before cooking the roast, season it on all sides with the seasoned salt. Transfer the roast to a pan. Cover with aluminum foil and refrigerate overnight.

2. Preheat the oven to 325°F. Position the oven rack in the lowest position possible.

3. Remove the roast from the refrigerator about 1 hour before roasting and allow to come to room temperature.

4. Cover the bottom of a large roasting pan with the rock salt to a depth of about $\frac{1}{2}$ inch. Put the roast on top of the rock salt and roast for $2\frac{1}{2}$ to 3 hours for medium-rare, or until the roast reaches the desired degree of doneness. The meat will be better done at the ends and rarer in the center.

5. Lift the roast from the pan and set it on a cutting board. Let the meat rest at room temperature for 15 to 20 minutes before carving. Loosely tent the roast with aluminum foil to keep it warm.

6. Remove the lip of the roast—the portion on top of the bones in front of the eye—and discard. Starting with the small end, carve the roast into thick pieces. To serve, spoon some of the Au Jus onto a plate, if desired. Put a slice of meat on top of the sauce. Repeat to make as many servings as needed. Serve the horseradish on the side.

Note: Rock salt is easy to find at hardware, housewares, and some grocery stores. You probably will need a little less than $4\frac{1}{2}$ pounds, but it's always better to buy more to ensure you have enough for your roasting pan.

CELEBRITY CLIP

In the more than ten years that they have been visiting Morton's steakhouses, Muhammad and Lonnie Ali have become friends of the restaurant, dining with us in so many of our locations. We welcome them most often at the Morton's in Louisville, Kentucky, Mr. Ali's birthplace and the home of the Muhammad Ali Center, which opened in November 2005. When contacted about our cookbook, Mr. Ali said, "Morton's is the place to go for great steak . . . every time, all the time."

CHOPPED STEAK

At the restaurant, we like big portions. But you might be more at ease cutting the amounts in half and making smaller patties. The secret is to use ground sirloin. Try to buy it from a butcher who will grind it in front of you, or who assures you that he grinds it at the store. Otherwise, buy good-looking ground meat from a market with high turnover. It should be a nice, rosy red without any graying or brown spots. Ground sirloin has less fat than other cuts but should still be evenly mixed with creamy-looking, small particles of fat. Look for ground beef with an 80:20 ratio of lean meat to fat.

WINE RECOMMENDATION: Red Zinfandel or Cabernet Sauvignon

SERVES 6

¼ cup **Clarified Butter** (page 231)
4 large **Spanish onions** (about 4 pounds),
   cut into 1-inch-square pieces
4 pounds medium-grind ground sirloin
¾ cup tomato juice
4 large eggs
1 tablespoon salt, plus more to taste
1 teaspoon freshly ground black pepper, plus more to taste
1½ teaspoons paprika
6 tablespoons Au Jus (optional; page 210)
1½ teaspoons chopped fresh curly-leaf parsley, for garnish

1. In a large skillet, melt the butter over medium heat. Add the onions and cook for 20 to 25 minutes, stirring often to prevent browning. The onions should soften but not color. Remove from the heat, cover, and set aside to keep warm.

2. Preheat the broiler and position the rack 4 inches from the heating element.

3. In a mixing bowl, mix the sirloin, tomato juice, eggs, 1 tablespoon salt, and 1 teaspoon pepper. Use your hands or a wooden spoon to mix thoroughly. Divide the meat into six equal portions. Shape into oval patties that are more flat than round. We do this on an oval plate. Transfer to a rack set on a baking sheet and round the edges of the patties so that they are even. You will need two racks and two baking sheets.

4. Broil the patties for about 8 minutes. Turn the patties and broil for another 8 minutes for medium-rare, or longer to the desired degree of doneness; for medium-done meat, that will be 8 to 10 minutes per side.

5. Meanwhile, reheat the onions in the same pan. Season with paprika and salt and pepper to taste.

6. Put a patty on each of six serving plates. Top with the sautéed onions and a tablespoon of Au Jus, if desired. Garnish the onions with chopped parsley.

MORTON'S HAMBURGERS

Years ago, before Arnie Morton and I really knew each other, we both worked at the Playboy Club in Montreal. We were in the process of changing the menu, and I cooked a hamburger that I sent out for Arnie to try. A few minutes later he burst into the kitchen, demanding in no uncertain terms to know "Who cooked that hamburger?" As I stepped forward to claim the distinction, I wasn't sure if Arnie was pleased or not. He exclaimed that it was the best he'd ever tasted. From that day forward, we worked together and eventually opened Morton's Steakhouses. So I have always called this the "Million-Dollar Hamburger"!

WINE RECOMMENDATION: Red Zinfandel

SERVES 6

- **4 pounds coarse-grind ground sirloin**
- **4 large eggs**
- **¾ cup tomato juice**
- **1 tablespoon salt**
- **1 teaspoon freshly ground black pepper**
- **6 large hamburger buns**
- **3 tablespoons Clarified Butter** (page 231)
- **Six ½-inch-thick slices tomato**
- **Six ¼-inch-thick slices Spanish onion**
- **6 large leaves iceberg lettuce**
- **Ketchup or another topping, for serving** (see Note; optional)

recipe continues

CELEBRITY CLIP

Frank Sinatra was a regular at Morton's. He loved our food and ambience and could count on us to respect his privacy. Nevertheless, he always traveled with a few bodyguards, who stood near his table. One night in 1982 or '83, he walked in with his friend Jack McHugh, a Chicago businessman. Sinatra asked for four bottles of his favorite wine, Château Pétrus. Raki Mehra, the maître d', checked the cellar and told the singer we had only three bottles on hand but could offer him a bottle of Château Lafite. When the check came several hours later, McHugh picked it up. The next day he called Raki and asked why the bill had been close to $4,000! Raki explained about the wine, and how Sinatra especially liked Château Pétrus. McHugh then asked Raki to buy him a case of the wine the next time he went to a wine auction so that he could send it to Sinatra.

1. Preheat the broiler. Lightly oil and position the rack as close to the heat source as possible.

2. In a mixing bowl, combine the sirloin, eggs, tomato juice, salt, and pepper. Use your hands or a wooden spoon to mix thoroughly. Divide the meat into six equal portions and gently form them into patties. Transfer to the broiler pan, and using a small sharp knife, make a crosshatch mark on the top of each burger about $\frac{1}{8}$ inch deep. (This lets the juices percolate through the burger, and we also like the way it looks.)

3. Brush the inside of each bun with butter. Toast the buns in the broiler for about 30 seconds on each side, or until lightly browned; be careful that the buns don't get too browned. Remove the buns and cover to keep warm. Reposition the broiler tray so that it is about 6 inches from the heat.

4. Broil the burgers for 3 to $3\frac{1}{2}$ minutes on each side for rare, 4 minutes on each side for medium-rare, and $4\frac{1}{2}$ to 5 minutes on each side for medium.

5. To serve, put the bottom half of each bun on a plate. Top with a burger and then a tomato slice, onion slice, and lettuce leaf. Add the top of the bun. Repeat to make five more burgers. Serve with ketchup, if desired.

Note: At the restaurant, we offer ketchup but also top the burgers with sautéed mushrooms (see the recipe for Wild Mushrooms with Garlic Butter on page 170), sautéed onions (see the recipe on page 118 for Chopped Steak), and all sorts of cheese, as requested—Cheddar, Monterey Jack, Swiss, and blue cheese are the most popular.

MORTON'S BEEF WELLINGTON

We like to think of this as a very contemporary beef Wellington. We use small, trimmed filets mignons, which cook evenly and relatively quickly, and frozen puff pastry, which is sold in every supermarket in the country. The chicken liver pâté filling is very similar to the Chicken Liver Pâté on page 66, so if you have some of that already made, use it instead. These are served as individual Wellingtons, rather than a big roast, and will absolutely delight your guests. And to make your life even easier, they can be assembled 2 to 3 hours ahead of time.

WINE RECOMMENDATION: Cabernet Sauvignon or Red Bordeaux

SERVES 6

Six 5-ounce filets mignons, about
    1½ inches thick
Salt and freshly ground black pepper
6 tablespoons Clarified Butter (page 231)
¾ cup Chicken Liver Pâté Filling
    (recipe follows)**, at room temperature**
¾ cup Duxelles (recipe follows)
1 sheet frozen puff pastry, thawed
¼ cup all-purpose flour
1 large egg
30 small whole shiitake mushrooms,
    trimmed as necessary
1½ cups Sauce Bordelaise (page 211)

recipe continues

1. Season the filets with salt and pepper to taste.

2. In a large sauté pan, heat 4 tablespoons of the Clarified Butter over high heat. When the butter is hot and smoking, sear the filets mignons for 1 to 2 minutes, or until lightly browned on one side. Turn and cook for 2 to 3 minutes longer, or until lightly browned on both sides. Transfer to a platter and set aside at room temperature to cool.

3. Put 2 tablespoons of the pâté on each cooled steak and spread over the surface but not all the way to the edge. Spread the Duxelles over the pâté.

4. Lay the puff pastry sheet on a lightly floured work surface and cut into six equal squares. Lightly dust each square with flour and then roll out each piece to 6 inches square, or large enough for the filet mignon.

5. In a small bowl, whisk together the egg with 2 tablespoons of water to make an egg wash.

6. Carefully invert a filet mignon into the center of each pastry square so that the Duxelles and pâté are on the bottom. Brush the edge of the pastry with a little egg wash, fold the pastry up over the sides of the steak, and pinch the edges together, pressing gently to seal.

recipe continues

DUXELLES
MAKES ABOUT ⅔ CUP

2 ounces cremini mushrooms, trimmed
2 ounces shiitake mushrooms, trimmed
2 ounces white button mushrooms, trimmed
1½ teaspoons Clarified Butter (page 231)
2 tablespoons minced shallots
¼ teaspoon minced garlic
¾ teaspoon finely chopped fresh thyme
Salt and freshly ground black pepper
1 tablespoon red wine

1. Using a sharp knife or in the bowl of a food processor fitted with a metal blade, finely chop all the mushrooms to a uniform size.

2. In a medium sauté pan, heat the butter over medium-low heat. Add the shallots and garlic and sauté for about 2 minutes, or until softened without browning.

3. Add the mushrooms and thyme, and season to taste with salt and pepper. Sauté for about 10 minutes, or until tender. Add the red wine and cook for 2 to 3 minutes, or until the wine has evaporated and the bottom of the skillet is dry. Transfer to a small bowl and set aside at room temperature to cool.

7. Transfer the pastry packets to a shallow, ungreased roasting pan large enough to hold all six in a single layer, sealed side down. Brush each Wellington with egg wash. Refrigerate for at least 1 hour and up to 4 hours.

8. Preheat the oven to 425°F.

9. Bake for about 25 minutes, or until the pastry is golden brown and the filets mignons are medium-rare. (If you have not refrigerated the Wellingtons before baking, reduce the cooking time by a few minutes.)

10. In a large sauté pan, heat the remaining 2 tablespoons of Clarified Butter over medium-high heat. Add the mushrooms and sauté for 8 to 10 minutes, or until the mushrooms are tender. Season to taste with salt and pepper.

11. To serve, put each Wellington in the center of each of six plates. Gently stir the mushrooms into the Sauce Bordelaise and reheat if necessary. Spoon the Sauce Bordelaise around each Wellington.

CELEBRITY CLIP

Queen Latifah celebrated her little sister's high school graduation with a party of twenty at Morton's Steakhouse at Riverside Square in Hackensack, New Jersey. She clearly enjoyed the filet mignon, Morton's salad, and our Legendary Hot Chocolate Cake, and everyone in the restaurant—guests and staff—had a great time! The singer must have found her meal fit for a queen because she came back two nights later.

CHICKEN LIVER PÂTÉ FILLING

MAKES ABOUT 1 CUP

$\frac{1}{2}$ pound fresh chicken livers

2 teaspoons Clarified Butter (page 231), plus more for covering the pâté

3 tablespoons chopped shallots

$2\frac{1}{4}$ teaspoons minced garlic

$\frac{3}{4}$ teaspoon finely chopped fresh thyme

4 teaspoons Port wine

6 tablespoons unsalted butter, softened

Pinch of allspice

Salt and freshly ground black pepper

1. Remove all the connective tissue and fat from the chicken livers. Put half of the cleaned livers in a mesh colander or similar strainer with a handle.

2. Bring a large pot of salted water to a boil. Reduce the heat so that the water is gently boiling. Submerge the colander holding half the livers in the boiling water and cook, uncovered, for 5 to 7 minutes to blanch, or until, when sliced, a liver is slightly pink in the center and not raw. The time depends on the size of the livers. Spread the blanched livers on a sheet pan. Let the water return to a boil and blanch the remaining chicken livers. Add them to the sheet pan. Refrigerate for at least 2 hours, or until completely cool.

3. In a large sauté pan, heat the Clarified Butter over low heat. Add the shallots, garlic, and thyme and sauté for 6 to 8 minutes, or until the shallots and garlic are tender.

4. Raise the heat to medium-high, add the Port, and cook for 3 to 4 minutes, or until most of the moisture evaporates. Remove from the heat and cool. Put the pan in the refrigerator and chill for at least 2 hours, or until completely cool.

5. In the bowl of a large food processor fitted with a metal blade, process the livers with the shallot mixture for about 1 minute, until blended and stiff. Add the butter and allspice and season to taste with salt and pepper. Process for 2 minutes longer, or until smooth and blended.

6. Line a shallow porcelain dish with plastic wrap, leaving a 3-inch overhang on two sides. Spoon the pâté into the dish and, using a rubber spatula, smooth the top. Tap the bowl gently on a work surface to remove any air pockets.

7. Cover the pâté with enough Clarified Butter to coat lightly. Fold the overhanging ends of the plastic wrap over the pâté and refrigerate for at least 6 hours or overnight to chill.

BEEF ROULADEN

This traditional German dish is even better if it's made a day or so ahead of time, refrigerated, and then heated. The flavors develop and mellow. Heat the rouladen slowly and then add the sour cream. When I was growing up in Germany, my mother made rouladen for Sunday dinner, especially if the pastor was coming. We had to sit quietly and behave ourselves at the table, but at least we had these little beef rolls as a reward, often served with mashed potatoes or spaetzle.

WINE RECOMMENDATION: Pinot Noir, Red Burgundy, or Merlot

SERVES 4

SAUCE
   ¼ **cup flavorless vegetable oil, such as canola or safflower**
   ¾ **cup chopped onions** (1 large onion)
   ½ **cup chopped celery** (1 medium rib)
   ½ **cup chopped carrots** (1 medium carrot)
   1 tablespoon tomato paste
   2 teaspoons all-purpose flour
   1 teaspoon hot Hungarian paprika
   ½ **cup red wine**
   2 cups canned beef or chicken broth
   2 bay leaves
   Salt and freshly ground black pepper
   ⅓ **cup sour cream**

ROULADEN
   ¼ **cup flavorless vegetable oil, such as canola or safflower**
   1½ **cups sliced yellow onions** (1 large or 2½ medium onions)
   Eight 4-ounce pieces top round beef (see Note)
   Salt and freshly ground black pepper
   2 tablespoons Dijon mustard
   4 slices bacon, halved crosswise
   Two 2½- to 3-inch-long dill pickles, quartered lengthwise
   ½ **cup canned beef broth**

recipe continues

1. To make the sauce, heat the oil in a flameproof casserole or small Dutch oven over medium-high heat. Sauté the onions, celery, and carrots for 3 to 4 minutes, or until the vegetables begin to soften. Add the tomato paste, flour, and paprika and cook, stirring, for about 3 minutes, or until well mixed and hot. Stir in the wine and bring to a boil. Add the broth and bay leaves, and bring back to a boil. Reduce the heat to low and simmer, partially covered, for about 10 minutes. Season to taste with salt and pepper. Set aside.

2. To make the rouladen, in a large, deep skillet, heat 2 tablespoons of the oil over medium-high heat. Cook the onions for 4 to 5 minutes, or until translucent. Remove from the heat until needed.

3. Using the flat side of a cleaver, a mallet, or a small, heavy frying pan, flatten each piece of beef so that it is about $\frac{1}{8}$ inch thick and about 8 inches long and 4 inches wide. Spread the meat on a work surface and season each slice with salt and pepper. Spread mustard over each and top each with an equal amount of the onions in the skillet (if you don't use all the onions, add them to the sauce). Put a piece of bacon and a pickle slice in the center of each slice, positioning them so that the bacon lies lengthwise along the meat and the pickle intersects the bacon in the middle of the meat (crosses it).

4. Starting at a short end, roll each piece of beef into a tight roll. Tie each roll with kitchen string or secure with toothpicks. Leave the rolls open at the ends; do not tuck in the ends.

5. In the same skillet, heat the remaining 2 tablespoons of oil over medium-high heat. Brown the rouladen for 1 to 2 minutes on each side so that they are evenly colored. Use tongs to turn them so that you don't pierce them. Using the tongs, transfer the rouladen to the reserved casserole of sauce.

6. Add the beef broth to the pan and bring to a boil over medium-high heat to deglaze the pan. Stir with a wooden spoon to scrape up the brown bits and to mix the onions with the broth. Add this mixture to the rouladen and the sauce.

7. Set the casserole over medium-high heat and bring the sauce to a boil. Reduce the heat to medium and simmer, partially covered, for about 40 minutes, turning the rouladen once, until the meat is thoroughly cooked and tender and the sauce thickens and clings to the rolls.

8. Lift the rouladen from the sauce and put them on a warm dish. Carefully remove the string or toothpicks. Remove and discard the bay leaves from the sauce.

9. Using an immersion blender, mix the sauce until smooth. (Alternatively, blend it in batches in a blender and return it to the casserole.) You will have about 3 cups of sauce. Return the rouladen to the sauce, season to taste with salt and pepper, and simmer for 5 minutes. Lift the rouladen from the sauce and put on a warm serving dish. (This can be made ahead of time and refrigerated. Refrigerate the rouladen separately from the sauce. Reheat the sauce before adding the sour cream.)

10. Stir the sour cream into the sauce and whisk until blended. Spoon the sauce over the rouladen and serve.

Note: Ask the butcher to slice the top round very thin. You could also look for beef round packaged as bracciole, which will be trimmed and thinly sliced.

CHICAGO PEPPER STEAK

We came up with this recipe in my adopted hometown of Chicago. I think it's a great dish because, as well as the steak, there are vegetables and rice and its flavors are slightly Asian. We make this with tenderloin. A whole trimmed tenderloin can weigh from 4 to 6 pounds, so for this recipe, where you need 24 ounces total, you will not need the entire tenderloin. Buy only what you need, or buy a whole tenderloin and freeze the remainder, well wrapped in plastic and then stored in a freezer-safe plastic bag for up to a month. Serve this pepper steak on individual plates, as we do at the restaurant, or put it on a serving plate and serve it family style. Either way, it's a hit.

WINE RECOMMENDATION: Shiraz, Syrah, or Rhone Valley Red

SERVES 6

3 large green bell peppers, seeded, ribs removed,
and cut into large chunks, each about 1½ inches square
1 to 1¼ Spanish onions, cut into large chunks (about 1 pound)
5 large plum tomatoes
1½ pounds beef tenderloin medallions, cut into 24 equal pieces,
each about 2 inches thick
Seasoned salt
¾ cup Clarified Butter (page 231)
10 to 12 large white mushrooms, trimmed and
sliced thick (about ¼ inch)
¼ cup Worcestershire sauce
¼ cup soy sauce
1¼ cups store-bought veal demi-glace (see Note, page 111)
1½ teaspoons cracked black peppercorns
6 to 8 cups Rice Pilaf (page 173)

1. Bring a large pot of lightly salted water to a boil. Blanch the green peppers and onions for about 2 minutes. Drain and immediately submerge in cold water. Drain again and set aside.

2. Core the tomatoes and cut in half lengthwise. Cut each half into four pieces. Set aside.

3. Season the medallions on all sides with seasoned salt to taste.

4. In a large sauté pan over high heat, heat the butter until very hot. Cook the pieces of beef for 45 seconds to 1 minute on each side, until browned but still rare, or until the desired degree of doneness. It may be necessary to cook the medallions in batches. Cut each in half against the grain and cover to keep warm.

5. Add the mushrooms and the blanched peppers and onions to the pan. Toss to combine.

6. In a small bowl, stir together the Worcestershire sauce and soy sauce.

7. Add the demi-glace, Worcestershire sauce–soy mixture, and peppercorns to the pan. Sauté for 1 to 2 minutes, or until the vegetables are hot. Add the tomatoes and bring to a boil. Stir to combine all the ingredients and cook for about 30 seconds.

8. To serve, arrange four pieces of beef on each of six plates and spoon the sauce over them. Serve with the pilaf on the side.

BEEF TENDERLOIN BROCHETTES WITH DIABLO SAUCE

This is an excellent way to use the end pieces of a filet. If you serve a whole filet and decide to cut off the narrow end, freeze the meat and then use it for these brochettes—everyone loves skewers packed with vegetables and beef cubes. Otherwise, use any part of the tenderloin or cubes of sirloin or another tender cut of beef. The Diablo Sauce is one of my all-time favorites, and is equally tasty with pork, chicken, or other steaks.

WINE RECOMMENDATION: Cabernet Sauvignon, Shiraz, Syrah, or Rhone Valley Red

SERVES 6

- 36 medium mushrooms
- 3 large green bell peppers, cut into a total of thirty
  1½-inch-square chunks
- 1 to 2 Spanish onions, cut into thirty
  1½-inch-square chunks
- 2 pounds beef tenderloin, cut into 30 equal pieces
- 3 tablespoons flavorless vegetable oil, such as
  canola or safflower
- Seasoned salt
- 6 plum tomatoes, halved
- 5 generous cups Rice Pilaf (page 173),
  for serving
- 2¼ cups Diablo Sauce (page 220)
- 6 watercress sprigs, for garnish

1. Preheat the broiler and position a rack 3 inches from the heating element.

2. Thread the mushrooms, peppers, onions, and beef onto six 15-inch metal skewers, beginning and ending with the mushrooms. So that everything cooks evenly, do not pack the food too tightly on the skewers. Brush with the oil and then season the brochettes generously with seasoned salt.

3. Broil the brochettes, turning to brown all sides, for 6 to 8 minutes total for medium-rare, 8 to 9 minutes for medium, or until the desired degree of doneness. Remove from the broiler and set aside.

4. Put the tomato halves on a broiler pan and broil for 4 to 5 minutes, or until softened and lightly browned.

5. To serve, put a little less than a cup of Rice Pilaf down the center of a plate. Ladle some of the Diablo Sauce on each side of the rice. Lay a skewer onto the rice and slide the meat and vegetables off the skewer on top of the rice. Arrange a tomato half at each end, and garnish with a sprig of watercress. Repeat to make five more servings.

CELEBRITY CLIP

One of the more celebrated regulars at our Orlando, Florida, steakhouse is Tiger Woods. When the golfer arrives, our staff generally seats him at "his booth"—booth 63—or, if he has requested it, in the restaurant's boardroom (the private dining room). Tiger usually arrives with his wife, who leads the way through the restaurant while he follows, baseball cap pulled down. Both staff and guests respect his desire for privacy. We were rewarded when Tiger invited fellow PGA tour member Mark O'Meara to join him one evening and both posed for photos with the Morton's managers.

ROMANIAN SKIRT STEAK WITH GOLDEN GARLIC AND FRIED PARSLEY

Skirt steak is delicious broiled, as in this recipe, grilled, or cooked in a very hot cast-iron skillet. While wildly versatile and full of flavor, it's a less expensive cut of meat sliced from the beef plate, and as such is not as tender as some other cuts. A lot of people marinate skirt steaks. We experimented with both marinated and nonmarinated, and surprisingly everyone preferred the nonmarinated meat. This recipe can also be made with tenderloin, but skirt steak is less expensive, easy to come by, and very tasty.

WINE RECOMMENDATION: Cabernet Sauvignon or Red Bordeaux

SERVES 6

1½ tablespoons olive oil
18 garlic cloves, peeled and left whole
¼ teaspoon salt, plus more for seasoning
   the parsley
Pinch of freshly ground black pepper
1 cup loosely packed curly-leaf parsley
   leaves (about ½ bunch)
Flavorless vegetable oil, such as
   canola or safflower
Three 16-ounce skirt steaks
Seasoned salt

1. In a small sauté pan, heat the olive oil over medium heat. When the oil is hot, sauté the garlic for about 6 minutes, or until golden brown and softened. Season with the salt and pepper. Remove from the heat and set aside until needed.

2. Remove the stems from the parsley. Wash and thoroughly dry the leaves.

3. Pour the vegetable oil into a heavy saucepan or high-sided skillet to a depth of about 1 inch (for a 10-inch skillet, you will need about 5 cups of oil). Heat over medium-high heat until shimmering hot. Using tongs, drop small batches of the parsley into the hot oil and fry for 15 to 20 seconds, or until shriveled and crispy. (Exercise caution because even a small amount of moisture on the parsley can cause the oil to spatter.) Lift from the hot oil with tongs and drain on a sheet pan lined with paper towels. Season very lightly with salt.

4. Preheat the broiler and position a rack about 4 inches from the heating element. Season the steaks on both sides with the seasoned salt. Broil for 3 minutes on each side for medium-rare; for medium, increase the time to 5 minutes on each side.

5. Garnish each plate with 3 garlic cloves and fried parsley.

LAMB CHOPS WITH BAKED APPLES

We serve double-cut loin lamb chops, which are thick and juicy. Look for good marbling in the eye (the thick piece of meat) and about $1/8$ inch of white fat on the outside of the chop. The fat should be firm and smooth. We buy American lamb from Colorado for this dish, but lamb from New Zealand or Australia is equally good. The chops should be frenched, which means the meat is trimmed about $1/2$ inch from the eye of the meat to the end of the bone. Most butchers will do this for you, and once you see it, it will look familiar.

WINE RECOMMENDATION: Pinot Noir, Red Burgundy, or Sangiovese

SERVES 6

3 firm, tart red apples, such as Red Delicious
3 tablespoons unsalted butter
Twelve 6-ounce double-cut loin lamb chops,
    each 1 to $1^1/2$ inches thick
$2^1/4$ teaspoons seasoned salt
Vegetable oil cooking spray
$1/4$ cup mint jelly

1. Preheat the oven to 450°F.

2. Cut the apples in half from top to bottom. Remove the stems and spoon out the cores. Cut off a thin slice from the rounded side of each half so that the apple halves lay flat. Transfer the apples, core side up, to a baking sheet.

3. Place $1^1/2$ teaspoons of butter in the center of each apple half. Bake, uncovered, for 15 to 25 minutes, depending on the firmness of the apples, until they begin to soften. Remove from the oven and set aside, covered with aluminum foil. (If you bake the apples ahead of time, reheat them in a 450°F. oven for 3 to 4 minutes, or until heated through.)

4. Remove the chops from the refrigerator 30 to 60 minutes before cooking. Lightly season both sides of the chops with seasoned salt.

5. Prepare a charcoal or gas grill or preheat the broiler and position a rack 4 inches from the heating element. Lightly spray the grill rack with vegetable oil cooking spray. The coals should be medium-hot for the charcoal grill. The burners should be on high for the gas grill.

6. If using a charcoal grill, grill the chops for 4 to 6 minutes. Turn, using tongs, and grill the other side for 5 to 6 minutes for medium-rare, or until the desired degree of doneness. If using a gas grill, grill the chops for 4 to 6 minutes. Turn, using tongs, and grill the other side for 5 to 6 minutes for medium-rare, or until the desired degree of doneness. If using the broiler, broil the lamb chops for 4 to 5 minutes per side for rare, 5 to 6 minutes per side for medium-rare, or until the desired degree of doneness.

7. Spoon 2 teaspoons of mint jelly into the center of each warm apple half and serve the apples alongside the lamb chops, two chops per serving.

BRAISED LAMB SHANKS WITH ROOT VEGETABLES AND MASHED POTATOES

Braised lamb shanks are welcoming and warm on cold winter days. This dish is not difficult to prepare, but it does take time, which is why I like to make these on weekends. As with most braises, this tastes even better when reheated a day or two after it's made. We use the whole shank, not one that is cut into pieces. Buy the size we recommend, which is not the largest sold; these smaller shanks are more tender.

WINE RECOMMENDATION: Pinot Noir, Red Burgundy, Sangiovese, or Tempranillo

SERVES 4

LAMB SHANKS

4 whole lamb shanks (about 4 pounds)
1 teaspoon garlic salt
1 teaspoon freshly ground black pepper
1/2 cup flavorless vegetable oil, such as canola or safflower
1 cup chopped celery (3 ribs)
1 cup chopped onion (1 medium to large onion)
1 cup chopped carrots (3 to 4 carrots)
2 tablespoons all-purpose flour
1/4 cup tomato paste
1/4 teaspoon dried oregano
1 cup red wine
2 tablespoons store-bought veal demi-glace (see Note, page 111)
2 bay leaves

ROOT VEGETABLES

2 to 3 carrots, trimmed and peeled
4 to 5 celery ribs, trimmed
4 tablespoons unsalted butter
24 canned and drained or frozen boiling onions (see Note)

6 cups Mashed Potatoes (page 179)
Chopped fresh curly-leaf parsley, for garnish

1. To prepare the lamb shanks, trim any excess fat from them and season with the garlic salt and pepper.

2. In a large stockpot or sauté pan, heat the oil over high heat until smoking. Add the lamb shanks and brown for about 5 minutes, turning to brown on all sides. Remove the shanks and set aside on a plate.

3. Reduce the heat to medium-high and add the chopped celery, onion, and carrots to the pan. Sauté for about 3 minutes, or until tender. Stir in the flour and mix well. Add the tomato paste and oregano, and cook, stirring, for about 1 minute, or until blended.

4. Add the red wine, demi-glace, and bay leaves, along with 3 cups of water. Bring to a boil. Return the lamb shanks to the pan, partially cover, and reduce the heat to low so that the liquid simmers gently. Cook for about 1 hour and 45 minutes, turning the shanks occasionally and stirring the sauce.

5. Remove the shanks from the sauce and transfer to a plate. Remove the bay leaves and discard. Using an immersion blender, blend the sauce for about 1 minute, or until smooth. (Alternatively, purée the sauce in a blender and then return it to the pan. You will have about 5 cups of puréed vegetables.) Return the shanks to the pan and simmer for about 20 minutes longer.

6. To prepare the root vegetables, roughly chop the carrots and celery into 1-inch pieces. In a large pot of lightly salted boiling water, blanch the carrots and celery for about 10 minutes, or until tender. Drain and immediately submerge in ice water. Drain again.

7. In a sauté pan, melt the butter over medium heat. Sauté the carrots, celery, and boiling onions for about 2 minutes, or until heated through.

8. To serve, put about 1½ cups Mashed Potatoes in the center of a shallow bowl. Put a lamb shank on top of the potatoes. Garnish with ¼ cup sautéed root vegetables and 6 boiling onions. Sprinkle the chopped parsley over the vegetables. Ladle the sauce over the meat and vegetables and repeat to make three more servings.

Note: If using frozen baby boiling onions, blanch them in boiling water for 3 to 5 minutes or according to the package directions. Drain and use as instructed in the recipe.

BROILED VEAL CHOPS

Veal chops are from the prime rib of a much younger animal and have far less marbling than mature beef. The meat should be pale white with a pink tinge, and all silver skin should be removed. Don't overcook veal chops—they are deliciously tender and sweet tasting but will dry out if overcooked.

WINE RECOMMENDATION: Pinot Noir, Red Burgundy, Merlot, or Beaujolais

SERVES 6

Six 12-ounce veal chops, each about
   1½ inches thick
Vegetable oil cooking spray
Seasoned salt
¾ cup Au Jus (optional; page 210)

1. Remove the veal chops from the refrigerator and let them rest at room temperature for 30 to 60 minutes.

2. Prepare a charcoal or gas grill or preheat the broiler and position a rack 4 inches from the heating element. Lightly spray the grill rack with vegetable oil cooking spray. The coals should be medium-hot for the charcoal grill. The burners should be on high for the gas grill.

3. Season the chops lightly on both sides with the seasoned salt. If using a charcoal grill, grill for 8 minutes. Turn, using tongs, and grill the other side for 7 to 8 minutes for medium-rare, or until the desired degree of doneness. If using a gas grill, grill for 8 minutes. Turn, using tongs, and grill the other side for 8 to 9 minutes for medium-rare, or until the desired degree of doneness. If using the broiler, broil about 4 inches from the heat source for 8 minutes. Turn, using tongs, and broil the other side for 7 to 8 minutes for medium-rare, or until the desired degree of doneness.

4. Spoon 2 tablespoons of Au Jus over each chop, if desired.

KLAUS'S WIENER SCHNITZEL

This old-world recipe originated in Vienna, Austria, although we Germans cook it just as well. Veal top round is an expensive cut, so my mother made this only on Sundays and special occasions. The veal should be cut thin and pan-fried right before serving, which means this is not a dish to make for more than four or six people. When my mother cooked it, she ladled the fat over the veal as it cooked so the meat crisped up a little.

WINE RECOMMENDATION: Riesling or Grüner Veltliner

SERVES 4

Eight 3½- to 4-ounce slices veal top round
Salt and freshly ground black pepper
2 large eggs
½ cup all-purpose flour
2½ cups fresh bread crumbs
½ cup unsalted butter
½ cup solid vegetable shortening, such as Crisco
2 lemons, halved, for garnish

1. Using the flat side of a cleaver, a mallet, or a small, heavy frying pan, flatten each piece of veal so that it is about ¼ inch thick. Season on both sides with salt and pepper.

2. In a small, shallow bowl, whisk the eggs with 2 tablespoons of water until smooth. Put the flour in another shallow bowl and the bread crumbs in a third.

3. Dip the veal slices first in the flour to coat both sides, next in the egg, and finally in the bread crumbs to coat well. Add another tablespoon of water to the egg if it seems thick. Set aside.

4. In a large, deep sauté pan, melt the butter and shortening over medium-high heat until liquid. In two or three batches, cook the breaded veal slices in the fat for about 2 minutes on each side, until golden brown. Turn once during cooking.

5. Serve immediately, garnished with lemon halves.

SICILIAN VEAL CHOPS

These chops are gently flavored with bread crumbs that have been mixed with a little Parmesan cheese and garlic to give them a taste of Italy. I don't think you want to flavor veal with anything more. The chops are best when treated with a light hand and cooked until medium-rare, no more.

WINE RECOMMENDATION: Merlot or Sangiovese

SERVES 6

Six 12-ounce veal chops, each about 1½ inches thick
Salt and freshly ground white pepper
¾ cup all-purpose flour
3 large eggs
2 cups Sicilian Bread Crumbs (recipe follows)
1½ cups Clarified Butter (page 231)
3 lemons, halved, for garnish
6 curly-leaf parsley sprigs, for garnish

SICILIAN BREAD CRUMBS
MAKES ABOUT 1½ CUPS

2 to 3 slices thick-cut white bread
(4 to 5 ounces)
½ cup (2 ounces) grated Parmesan cheese
1¾ teaspoons garlic powder
¾ teaspoon freshly ground white pepper

1. Slice the crusts from the bread and then cut the bread into large chunks.

2. In the bowl of a food processor fitted with a metal blade, grind the bread to fine crumbs. You should have about 1 cup of crumbs.

3. Transfer the bread crumbs to a small mixing bowl. Add the Parmesan, garlic powder, and pepper. Mix well. Use right away or refrigerate in a tightly covered storage container for 2 to 3 days.

1. Gently pound the veal chops with a meat mallet or a small, heavy skillet to soften. They have a bone so will not flatten. Pat the meat dry with paper towels and then season on both sides with salt and pepper.

2. Spread the flour on a plate. In a medium bowl, whisk the eggs with 3 tablespoons of water. Spread the bread crumbs on another plate.

3. Dredge the chops in the flour, shaking off any excess. Dip the chops in the egg wash, letting any excess drip back into the bowl. Coat the chops with the bread crumbs. Let the breaded chops rest at room temperature for about 10 minutes.

4. Preheat the oven to 450°F.

5. In a large nonstick sauté pan, heat ¾ cup of the butter over medium heat. When hot, add three veal chops. Cook on each side for 2 to 3 minutes, or until golden brown. Using a spatula, transfer to a baking sheet lined with foil. Repeat with the remaining veal chops, using more butter as necessary.

6. Transfer to the oven and bake for 8 minutes. Turn the chops over and bake for an additional 6 or 7 minutes, or until medium-rare.

7. Remove from the oven. Garnish each chop with a lemon half and a sprig of parsley.

CELEBRITY CLIP

Arnie Morton's, our restaurant in Burbank, California, is just minutes from some of the most powerful seats of the entertainment business. The studios for NBC's **Tonight Show**, Warner Brothers Studios, and Disney's executive offices are practically around the corner. Over the years we've welcomed Jay Leno, Katie Couric, and Jeff Zucker from NBC; movie and television stars George Clooney, Jennifer Garner, and Ray Romano; and Disney heavyweights (past and present) Jeffrey Katzenberg and Michael Eisner.

CHICKEN CHRISTOPHER

I like this chicken dish because of the garlic! It's named for our corporate chef, Chris Rook, who came up with it several years ago. Chris is involved whenever we open a new restaurant, and therefore we spend a lot of time together. He is trained in classic French cooking, and I find it a joy to cook with him. This dish is tender and light; the trick is to pound the chicken just enough that the pieces are uniformly thin and cook evenly and quickly.

WINE RECOMMENDATION: Riesling

SERVES 6

$4\frac{1}{2}$ **pounds skinless, boneless chicken breasts**
1 cup all-purpose flour
3 large eggs
3 to 4 cups Alex's Bread Crumbs (page 232)
Salt and freshly ground white pepper
$2\frac{1}{4}$ **cups Clarified Butter** (page 231)
2 tablespoons chopped shallots
2 tablespoons minced garlic
3 cups Beurre Blanc (page 216)
3 tablespoons chopped fresh curly-leaf parsley

1. Cut the chicken breasts into eighteen 4-ounce pieces. (Slightly smaller pieces are acceptable if it's tricky to cut as many 4-ounce pieces as you need.) Cover the chicken breasts with waxed paper or plastic wrap. Using a meat mallet or the bottom of a small skillet, gently flatten the breasts to an even thickness of about $1/2$ inch.

2. Spread the flour on a plate. In a medium bowl, whisk the eggs with $1/3$ cup of water. Spread the bread crumbs on another plate. Pat the chicken pieces dry with paper towels and season with salt and pepper. Dredge with the flour, shaking off any excess, then dip the chicken in the egg wash, letting any excess drip back into the bowl. Coat the chicken completely with the bread crumbs. Set aside on a tray or large plate.

3. In a large sauté pan, melt $1^{1}/_{2}$ cups of the butter over medium heat. Add the chicken and cook for about $1^{1}/_{2}$ minutes on each side, or until golden brown and crisp. Transfer to a plate and keep warm. Do not overcrowd the pan while sautéing the chicken.

4. In another large sauté pan, melt the remaining $3/4$ cup butter over medium heat and sauté the shallots and garlic for 1 to 2 minutes, or until translucent. Add the Beurre Blanc and parsley, and stir well. Remove the sauce from the heat and season to taste with salt and pepper.

5. Serve the chicken with the sauce on the side.

BAKED LEMON-OREGANO CHICKEN

Lemon and oregano are a good team, particularly when paired with chicken. I like the slight tang provided by the lemon juice, which complements the other ingredients perfectly. When you want a fresh-tasting chicken dish, this is a great choice.

WINE RECOMMENDATION: Chardonnay or White Burgundy

SERVES 6

Three 2½-pound chickens (see Note)
2 tablespoons dried oregano
1 tablespoon salt
1½ teaspoons garlic powder
1½ teaspoons freshly ground white pepper
Juice of 3 lemons (about ¾ cup), **plus 3 lemons,
   halved, for garnish**
3 cups coarsely chopped red onions
   (1 pound onions)
6 curly-leaf parsley sprigs, for garnish

1. Ask the butcher to cut the chickens along each side of the backbone. Remove and discard the backbones. Remove the wing tips and discard.

2. In a small bowl, mix the oregano, salt, garlic powder, and white pepper. Sprinkle half the mixture over the chickens and then drizzle with half the lemon juice. Rub into the chickens. Turn the chickens over and repeat with the remaining herbs and spices and lemon juice.

recipe continues

3. Sprinkle the onions over two small, shallow, nonreactive baking pans. Lay the chickens, skin side up, on top of the onions. Add enough cold water to the baking pans to cover the bottoms to a depth of about $\frac{1}{4}$ inch. Cover with plastic wrap and refrigerate for at least 4 hours or overnight.

4. Preheat the oven to 450°F.

5. Remove the chickens from the refrigerator and let them rest on the counter for about 20 minutes to reach room temperature. Turn the chickens over so that they are skin side down and bake for about 10 minutes. Turn and bake for 20 minutes longer, or until golden brown and cooked through.

6. Remove the rib bones and the bones connected to the thigh bones. Or, if this is too difficult, halve or quarter the chickens for serving. Cover and set aside to keep warm.

7. In a small saucepan, heat $\frac{1}{2}$ cup of the pan juices and onions over medium-high heat until hot. Spoon over the chickens, and garnish each serving with a lemon half and a sprig of parsley.

Note: These are small chickens and while they are not hard to find, you may have to ask the butcher for them or even special-order them. Buy the smallest you can find and don't worry too much about the exact weight. Young chickens are tender.

BROILED LEMON CHICKEN WITH LINGUINI

Not surprisingly, we don't serve many pasta dishes at Morton's. But that doesn't mean we don't know great pasta. This creamy, lemony chicken is wonderful spooned over linguini. Here's a trick: always save a little pasta cooking water and use it to thin or extend a sauce. It's a little starchy and much better than plain water.

WINE RECOMMENDATION: Pinot Grigio or Sauvignon Blanc

SERVES 6

3 tablespoons flavorless vegetable oil,
    such as canola or safflower
2 pounds linguini
¾ pound fresh or frozen pea pods (12 ounces)
2¼ pounds boneless, skinless chicken breasts,
    cut into 12 equal pieces
1½ teaspoons seasoned salt
Juice of 3 lemons (about ¾ cup), plus 3 lemons,
    halved, for garnish
3¾ cups Cream Sauce (page 215)
6 curly-leaf parsley sprigs, for garnish

1. Bring a large pot of lightly salted water and the oil to a boil. Add the pasta and cook, stirring occasionally, for 9 to 10 minutes, or until al dente. Ladle 1 cup of the pasta cooking water from the pot and set aside. Drain the pasta and immediately submerge it in cold water. Drain again and set aside.

2. Bring a small saucepan of lightly salted water to a boil. Blanch the pea pods for 2 to 3 minutes if fresh and about 1 minute if frozen, or until just tender. Drain and immediately submerge in cold water. Drain again. Cut the pea pods into thin slices or julienne and reserve.

recipe continues

3. Preheat the broiler and position a rack 3 inches from the heating element.

4. Spread the chicken pieces on a broiler pan; season on all sides with seasoned salt and drizzle with lemon juice. Broil the chicken, turning at least once, for about 10 minutes, or until cooked through and tender. Set aside, covered, to keep warm.

5. Transfer the cooked linguini to a large nonstick sauté pan and heat over medium heat, tossing to prevent sticking. Add the Cream Sauce and the pea pods, toss to combine, and cook until heated through. Add as much of the reserved pasta water as needed to thin the sauce to the consistency you like; start by adding 2 to 3 tablespoons.

6. Divide the pasta among six dinner plates. Slice each piece of chicken on a diagonal into three to four slices, each about ⅜ inch thick. Fan out on top of the pasta. Garnish each plate with a lemon half and a sprig of parsley.

CELEBRITY CLIP

Even musicians from the Woodstock generation know a good steak when they taste one. During a recent tour, David Crosby, Stephen Stills, and Graham Nash, who as Crosby Stills and Nash—and frequently Crosby Stills Nash and Young—lit up the California music scene in the 1960s and '70s, got together at our Phoenix restaurant. Each musician ordered a 24-ounce porterhouse steak and they all seemed to have a great time. Ironically, about a week later, who should show up for dinner at Morton's Steakhouse in Pittsburgh? None other than Neil Young!

BAKED LOBSTER WITH CREAM

Maine lobsters are delicious steamed or boiled, but we like them baked for the texture and presentation. We serve very large lobsters and suggest you buy good-size ones for this recipe. It's for one serving, but if there are two or more guests, you may find one large lobster is ample for your needs, or simply double everything. Always buy live lobsters—it's the only guarantee of freshness. A word of warning: when we tested this in a home kitchen for this book, it smoked and even set off the smoke alarm! Turn on the exhaust fan before you begin.

WINE RECOMMENDATION: Chardonnay or White Burgundy

SERVES 1

One 3- to 5-pound live Maine lobster
2 tablespoons heavy cream
7 tablespoons hot Clarified Butter (page 231)
½ lemon, for garnish

1. Preheat the oven to 450°F.

2. Remove the claws from the lobster and crack with the back of the knife (see Note). Set aside the claws. Split the body in half and remove the small stomach sacs behind the eyes of the lobster (these are obvious when you open the lobster; by splitting the lobster in half you will cut the sac in half, too). Arrange the lobster and the claws in a shallow baking pan, split side up, and add the cream to the body's cavity, being sure to cover any roe. Drizzle the tail with 2 tablespoons of the butter.

3. Bake for 15 to 20 minutes, depending on the size of the lobster, until the shell turns bright red and the lobster meat is opaque. Transfer the baked lobster to a plate. Garnish with the lemon half. Serve with the remaining 5 tablespoons of butter in a small bowl alongside the lobster. (If serving two people, increase the amount of butter for dipping.)

Note: Before removing the claws, insert a small, sharp knife into the lobster at the back of its head. This will sever the nervous system immediately.

SHRIMP ALEXANDER WITH BEURRE BLANC

This can be a main course, an appetizer, or finger food at a cocktail party, with or without the Beurre Blanc. When I went to Germany recently for my sister's birthday, I carried frozen shrimp in my suitcase so that I could make this for the party. Everyone loved it. Make sure the butter is warm when you dip the shrimp in it.

WINE RECOMMENDATION: Chardonnay, Chablis, or Pinot Grigio

SERVES 6

18 fresh large shrimp (8/11 count), **shells on**
1 cup warm Clarified Butter (page 231)
1½ cups Alex's Bread Crumbs (page 232)
1½ cups Beurre Blanc (page 216)
3 lemons, halved, for garnish

1. Preheat the oven to 450°F.

2. Peel the shrimp as far as the tail; leave the tail shell intact. Devein the shrimp and rinse well. With a small, sharp knife, cut open the shrimp along the vein line approximately two-thirds of the way through the shrimp.

3. Put the warm melted butter in one shallow bowl or deep plate and the bread crumbs in another. (Glass pie plates also work well.) Dip a shrimp in the butter and let the butter drip off the shrimp. Dip the shrimp in the crumbs and press the crumbs on the shrimp so that it is completely coated. Put the shrimp on a cutting board, cut side down, and press slightly to flatten and form a base so that the shrimp can stand upright. Bring the tail over the shrimp and insert the point between the tail fins into the thick end of the shrimp. Repeat with the remaining shrimp.

4. As each shrimp is prepared, set it, cut side down, on a foil-lined baking sheet. Pour any remaining butter over the shrimp. Bake the shrimp for 12 to 13 minutes, or until cooked through and the bread crumbs are crisp and lightly brown.

5. Spoon ¼ cup of Beurre Blanc on each of six serving plates. Top with three shrimp and garnish each plate with a lemon half.

SWORDFISH WITH BÉARNAISE SAUCE

Although we're a steakhouse, we have guests who like fish now and then, and meaty swordfish holds up to our rich, velvety Béarnaise Sauce. Swordfish is wonderful on the grill or under the broiler. Beyond buying the freshest fish you can find, look for swordfish that is juicy, firm, and meaty.

WINE RECOMMENDATION: Chardonnay or White Burgundy

SERVES 6

Vegetable oil cooking spray
Six 8- to 10-ounce swordfish steaks, each 1$\frac{1}{4}$ to 1$\frac{1}{2}$ inches thick
About 6 teaspoons flavorless vegetable oil,
    such as canola or safflower, for brushing
3 teaspoons seasoned salt
3 lemons, halved, for garnish
6 curly-leaf parsley sprigs, for garnish
1$\frac{1}{2}$ cups Béarnaise Sauce (page 214)

1. Preheat the broiler or prepare a charcoal or gas grill. Lightly spray the grill rack with vegetable oil cooking spray. The coals or heating element should be medium-hot.

2. Lightly brush both sides of the swordfish with oil and lightly season on both sides with seasoned salt. Broil or grill the fish for 6 minutes. Turn and grill for 4 to 6 minutes longer, depending on the thickness of the fish, or until the center is slightly opaque and beginning to flake.

3. Put the fish on a serving platter and garnish with lemon halves and parsley. Spoon the sauce over the fish or serve it on the side.

SALMON WITH BEURRE BLANC

Salmon is best served simply, as we do here, with no more accompaniment than our Beurre Blanc. Salmon is widely available, in part because so much of it is farmed, and it has become wildly popular. Look for pink-to-orange coloring and relatively firm texture. Broiling or grilling the fillets in the skin keeps them intact and adds rich, luxuriant flavor. We could serve with our Béarnaise Sauce (page 214) just as deliciously as with the Beurre Blanc—or with only a squeeze of lemon juice.

WINE RECOMMENDATION: Chardonnay or White Burgundy

SERVES 6

Vegetable oil cooking spray
Six 8- to 10-ounce salmon fillets, with skin, if possible
1/3 cup flavorless vegetable oil, such as canola or safflower
1 tablespoon seasoned salt
3 lemons, halved, for garnish
1 1/2 cups Beurre Blanc (page 216)

1. Preheat the broiler or prepare a charcoal or gas grill. Lightly spray the grill rack with vegetable oil cooking spray. The coals or heating element should be medium-hot.

2. Lightly brush both sides of the salmon fillets with oil and then season both sides lightly with seasoned salt. If using the oven, broil the salmon, skin side down, about 3 inches from the heat source for about 5 minutes. Slide a spatula between the skin and the fish and turn the fish over. Broil the salmon for 3 to 5 minutes longer, or until opaque and beginning to flake. If grilling, place it on the grate, skin side down, for about 5 minutes. Turn and grill for 3 to 5 minutes more.

3. Serve each fillet garnished with a lemon half. Serve the Beurre Blanc on the side.

BAKED COD WITH ALEX'S BREAD CRUMBS

Lightly coating a mild fish such as cod with bread crumbs makes it crunchy on the outside and moist and tender on the inside. You could use another firm-fleshed white fish, such as snapper or halibut.

WINE RECOMMENDATION: Chardonnay or White Burgundy

SERVES 6

Six 8- to 10-ounce cod fillets, each about ¾ inch thick
Seasoned salt
½ cup warm Clarified Butter (page 231)
About 1½ cups Alex's Bread Crumbs (page 232) **or enough to coat the fish**
1½ cups Beurre Blanc (page 216)
3 lemons, halved, for garnish
6 curly-leaf parsley sprigs, for garnish

1. Preheat the oven to 450°F.

2. Season the cod with the seasoned salt. Put the warm butter in a shallow dish and the bread crumbs in another shallow dish. Dip the bright white side of the fillets in the butter and then press the butter side into the bread crumbs to coat lightly.

3. Put the cod, breaded side up, in a shallow baking pan. Bake for 12 to 13 minutes, or until the fish is translucent in the center. The cooking time will depend on the thickness of the fillets.

4. Ladle some Beurre Blanc in the center of six serving plates and set a cod fillet on top of the sauce. Garnish each plate with a lemon half and a parsley sprig.

FLORIDA GROUPER WITH TOMATOES

When you buy fish, whether it's grouper for this recipe or the fish for any other recipe in the book, try to get it from a busy merchant with good turnover. Avoid fish that has any odor other than a clean, briny one, and if you can't find good fresh fish, buy flash-frozen fish. But stay away from any fish that has been frozen and then allowed to thaw before it's sold. Cook fish the day you buy it (or the next day at the latest) and store it on a bed of crushed ice in the refrigerator. The fishmonger will give you some crushed ice if you ask.

WINE RECOMMENDATION: Chardonnay or White Burgundy

SERVES 6

Six 8- to 10-ounce grouper fillets, each about 1 to 1½ inches thick
Seasoned salt
¾ cup flavorless vegetable oil, such as canola or safflower
¾ cup chopped tomatoes (3 plum tomatoes)
¾ cup Beurre Blanc (page 216)
3 lemons, halved, for garnish
6 curly-leaf parsley sprigs, for garnish

1. Preheat the oven to 450°F.

2. Season the grouper with the seasoned salt and coat lightly with vegetable oil. Arrange the fillets in a shallow baking pan and top with the chopped tomatoes. Bake for 17 to 18 minutes, or until the fillets are translucent in the center. (For thinner fillets, the cooking time will be closer to 12 to 14 minutes.)

3. Ladle some Beurre Blanc in the center of six serving plates and set a grouper fillet on top of the sauce, tomato side up. Garnish each plate with a lemon half and a parsley sprig.

LINGUINI WITH CLAMS AND SHRIMP

Clams and shrimp tossed with pasta is a wonderful, quick supper. When you buy fresh clams, make sure all are closed. Hold them on ice until you are ready to cook them, which should be the same day you purchase them.

WINE RECOMMENDATION: Pinot Grigio or Sauvignon Blanc

SERVES 6

2 tablespoons flavorless vegetable oil,
such as canola or safflower
2 pounds linguini
12 tablespoons (1½ sticks) **unsalted butter**
30 littleneck clams (4½ pounds)**, rinsed and scrubbed**
2 tablespoons chopped garlic
2 tablespoons chopped green onion, white parts only
3 cups dry white wine
2¼ cups bottled clam juice
12 large shrimp (21/25 count)**, peeled and deveined**
2 tablespoons chopped fresh curly-leaf parsley,
plus more for garnish
3 tablespoons diced tomato (1 plum tomato, seeded)
Grated Parmesan cheese, for serving

1. Add the oil to a large pot of lightly salted water and bring to a boil over high heat. Add the pasta and cook, stirring occasionally, for 9 to 10 minutes, or until al dente. Drain and immediately submerge in cold water. Drain again and set aside.

2. In the same large pot, melt the butter over medium heat. Add the clams, garlic, and green onion. Sauté for 30 seconds. Add the wine and clam juice. Cover the pan and steam the clams, shaking occasionally, for 3 to 4 minutes, or until the clams start to open. Add the shrimp and parsley, and cover the pan. Steam for 3 to 4 minutes longer, or until the clams have all opened and the shrimp are pink and cooked through. Discard any clams that do not open.

3. Add the linguini and diced tomato to the pan and toss well. Cover and cook for 2 to 3 minutes to heat through. Using tongs, divide the linguini among six shallow pasta bowls and arrange the clams and shrimp on top. Garnish the pasta with chopped parsley and serve with grated Parmesan.

CELEBRITY CLIP

Everyone who knows the Chicago Morton's on State Street knows our maître d', Raki Mehra, who has been there for twenty-six years. If you don't, look at the wall with our celebrity pictures. Raki is the guy smoking a cigar alongside Steven Tyler of Aerosmith. He's also the guy standing next to Michael Jordan (Raki is the shorter one!).

7

SIDE DISHES

Creamed Spinach

Sautéed Spinach and Mushrooms

Wild Mushrooms with Garlic Butter

Mushrooms and Onions

Rice Pilaf

Hash Brown Potatoes

Potato Skins

Herbed New Potatoes

Mashed Potatoes

Lyonnaise Potatoes

CREAMED SPINACH

Home cooks have been making creamed spinach forever, and because we receive so many requests for it at the restaurant, we put it on the menu a few years ago. And none too soon; it's ordered more than any other side dish. We've adapted this for the home kitchen so that you'll have success every time!

SERVES 6 TO 8

¼ cup (½ stick) **unsalted butter**
¾ **cup minced yellow onion**
1¼ **tablespoons minced garlic**
2 **teaspoons seasoned or coarse salt**
1 **teaspoon freshly ground black pepper**
¾ **teaspoon freshly grated nutmeg**
¼ **cup all-purpose flour**
3½ **cups half-and-half**
2¼ **pounds chopped frozen spinach, thawed and squeezed dry**
⅓ **cup freshly grated Parmesan cheese** (1¾ ounces)

1. In a large saucepan, melt the butter over medium-low heat. Add the onion and garlic, and sauté for about 10 minutes, or until the onion is translucent. Stir in the salt, pepper, and nutmeg.

2. Sprinkle the flour over the onion and cook over low heat, stirring with a wooden spoon, for about 4 minutes, or until there is a nutty aroma. Add the half-and-half and cook over medium-low heat, whisking occasionally, until hot. Raise the heat to medium-high and bring to a boil. Whisk continuously for 6 to 8 minutes, or until the mixture thickens.

3. Remove the pan from the heat. Using a handheld immersion blender, blend the sauce for 1 to 2 minutes, or until smooth. Stir in the spinach until well mixed and heated through. Serve immediately or cover and set aside to keep warm.

4. Just before serving, set the pan over medium heat. Add the Parmesan and stir until the cheese is mixed in and the spinach is heated through. Adjust the seasonings, if necessary.

SAUTÉED SPINACH AND MUSHROOMS

When I dine at Morton's, I always order this side dish. It's my all-time favorite. When I make it at home, I don't always blanch the spinach first but instead add it raw to the pan and cook it that way. For the best results, I suggest you blanch it, especially if you want to do some of the prep work ahead of time. Be sure to squeeze out as much moisture as you possibly can; otherwise the final dish could be a little watery. Sometimes I top it with a sliced Granny Smith apple.

SERVES 6

30 ounces raw spinach, stems removed (see Note)
12 tablespoons ($1^{1}/_{2}$ sticks) **unsalted butter**
20 ounces medium white mushrooms, cut into $^{1}/_{4}$**-inch-thick slices** (about 6 cups)
2 shallots, chopped (about 3 tablespoons)
Salt and freshly ground white pepper
Generous pinch of sugar

1. In a large pot of boiling water, blanch the spinach for about 45 seconds or until wilted. Drain and immediately submerge in cold water. Drain again. Wrap the spinach in a clean kitchen towel and squeeze out as much of the moisture as you can. Set aside.

2. In a large nonstick sauté pan, melt the butter over medium heat. When the butter is bubbling, add the mushrooms and shallots, and season with salt and pepper to taste. Sauté for 5 to 6 minutes, or until the vegetables begin to soften and brown lightly.

3. Add the spinach, sprinkle with the sugar, and sauté for about 3 minutes, or until the spinach is a little more wilted, heated through, and well mixed with the mushrooms and shallots.

Note: Three 10-ounce bags of whole spinach leaves (not baby spinach) are perfect here. If your supermarket or greengrocer packs spinach in bags of different weights or sells it loose, anything between 25 and 35 ounces will work well.

WILD MUSHROOMS WITH GARLIC BUTTER

The name of this recipe is a misnomer because we use cultivated, farm-raised mushrooms. The term **wild** is applied to these specialty mushrooms to differentiate them from more common white mushrooms. Cook these mushrooms as soon as you can—they don't store well—and clean them first. The best way to clean them is to wipe them with a damp cloth or to use a soft mushroom brush. When you clean the portobellos, scrape away the dark gills on the underside with a spoon and slice off the stems. The hardest part of this recipe? In my opinion, it's preparing the Garlic Butter! But that can be made well ahead of time and frozen to be ready when you are.

SERVES 6

    6 slices very thin white bread
    6$\frac{1}{2}$ ounces portobello mushrooms
    4$\frac{1}{2}$ ounces shiitake mushrooms
    6 ounces cremini mushrooms
    $\frac{3}{4}$ cup Garlic Butter (page 224)

1. Preheat the oven to 400°F.

2. Lay the bread slices out on a work surface. Using a 3-inch round cookie cutter or water glass, cut out six rounds. (Discard the crusts and trimmings or use them for bread crumbs.) Transfer the rounds to a baking sheet. Bake for 2 to 3 minutes, or until the toast rounds are light golden brown and crisp. Cool on wire racks.

3. Twist or cut the stems off the portobello and shiitake mushrooms. With a spoon, scrape the gills out of the portobellos. Discard the stems or reserve for another use. Cut all the mushrooms into $\frac{1}{4}$-inch-wide slices.

4. Heat a large sauté pan over medium heat until warm. Add the Garlic Butter, and when it's melted, raise the heat to medium-high. Add the mushrooms, and sauté for 5 to 7 minutes, or until the mushrooms release their liquid and are softened.

5. Spoon the mushroom mixture in equal amounts onto each toast and serve.

MUSHROOMS AND ONIONS

There is nothing to this one! Put everything in the pan, and in 20 or 25 minutes you have a lovely little side dish. You can easily double this. Use ordinary white mushrooms or slightly more flavorful cremini. Both are easy to find.

SERVES 6

$\frac{1}{2}$ **cup (1 stick) unsalted butter**
3 cups thinly sliced Spanish onions (about 1 pound)
14 to 16 ounces white or cremini mushrooms, sliced (about $4\frac{1}{2}$ cups)
$\frac{3}{4}$ **cup Au Jus** (optional; page 210)
Salt and freshly ground white pepper
2 tablespoons chopped fresh curly-leaf parsley

1. In a large sauté pan, melt the butter over medium heat. Add the onions and sauté for 8 to 10 minutes, or until golden brown. Add the mushrooms and sauté for 5 to 6 minutes, or until the mushrooms release their liquid and are softened.

2. Add the Au Jus, if desired, bring to a simmer, and cook for 8 to 10 minutes, or until the liquid has almost evaporated. Season to taste with salt and pepper. Stir in the parsley and serve hot.

RICE PILAF

Some meals call for rice, such as the Beef Tenderloin Brochettes with Diablo Sauce (page 134) or the Florida Grouper with Tomatoes (page 161). I feel that when you cook rice, it's so easy to dress it up and make a pilaf, why not? It tastes better than plain rice.

SERVES 8

1 tablespoon unsalted butter
2½ tablespoons small-diced Spanish onion
1¼ tablespoons small-diced red bell pepper
1¼ tablespoons small-diced green bell pepper
2½ tablespoons chicken base (see Note)
3½ cups hot water
¾ pound long-grain rice
1 teaspoon chopped fresh curly-leaf parsley

1. Preheat the oven to 400°F.

2. In a small sauté pan, melt the butter over medium heat. Add the onion and red and green peppers, and sauté for about 5 minutes, or until the vegetables soften.

3. In a large bowl, dissolve the chicken base in the hot water. Transfer to a 1-quart casserole and add the rice and sautéed vegetables. Bake, uncovered, for about 30 minutes, or until the liquid is absorbed and the rice is tender. Garnish with the chopped parsley and serve.

Note: You can buy chicken base in supermarkets. For instance, Bear Creek brand is sold in 8-ounce containers in the soup aisle. Or you can order it online at www.bearcreekfoods.com.

HASH BROWN POTATOES

These are absolutely wonderful, although I sometimes think agreeing to serve them in the restaurant was one of my biggest mistakes. They are labor-intensive because you need to grate the potatoes properly, wash them so that the water runs clear, squeeze the potatoes dry, and make very sure the seasoning is well distributed when you mix them. After that, making these sizeable potato cakes is a breeze! You may want to halve this recipe; you'll still have enough to serve six, particularly if you serve a few other side dishes.

SERVES 6

6 pounds russet potatoes, such as Idaho, scrubbed and rinsed (see Note)
1½ teaspoons salt
¼ teaspoon freshly ground white pepper
3 cups Clarified Butter (page 231)

1. Preheat the oven to 450°F.

2. Shred the potatoes, with the skins, on the large holes of a box grater into a large mixing bowl. You should have about $11\frac{1}{4}$ cups shredded potatoes. Put the shredded potatoes in a large bowl and fill it with cold water. Drain and repeat until the water runs clear. Wrap the potatoes in a dish towel and pat dry, or dry by spinning the potatoes in a salad spinner. Transfer to a mixing bowl. Season the potatoes with the salt and pepper, or more to taste.

3. In a 10-inch nonstick sauté pan, heat $\frac{1}{2}$ cup of the butter over medium-high heat. Add approximately one-sixth (less than 2 cups) of the shredded potatoes to the pan. Using a spatula, shape the potatoes into a round large enough to fill the pan. Do not press down on the potatoes. Cook, occasionally shaking the pan, for 5 to 6 minutes, or until the bottom is golden brown. Turn with a spatula, level the top, and cook for 3 to 4 more minutes, or until golden brown on both sides. Lift the pancake from the pan and transfer to a wire rack to drain. Repeat to make five more hash browns.

4. Transfer the hash browns, still on the rack, to a baking sheet. Transfer to the oven and bake for 4 to 5 minutes, or until heated through.

Note: There is a short time every year, usually at the end of the summer, when potatoes are too fresh to make hash browns. This may sound counterintuitive, but for a few weeks every September, we find the potatoes are too moist.

POTATO SKINS

When done right, these are outstanding. The trick is to use large potatoes, so you have enough skin to work with, and to leave just the right amount of potato flesh on the skins. These turn out crisp and tasty and can be served as they come from the oven or with sour cream, chopped bacon, minced onions, and shredded Cheddar—or your favorite filling.

SERVES 6

6 large russet potatoes (each 8 to 10 ounces)
3 tablespoons unsalted butter, melted
Salt and freshly ground white pepper
Chopped fresh curly-leaf parsley, for garnish

1. Preheat the oven to 400°F.

2. Scrub the potatoes and prick them in several places with a fork. Lay on the center rack of the oven and bake for 1 hour to 1 hour and 20 minutes, or until the potatoes are cooked through and feel tender when pierced with a small sharp knife. Remove from the oven and set aside to cool.

3. Increase the oven temperature to 450°F.

4. When the fully cooked potatoes are cool enough to handle, cut each in half lengthwise. Scoop out most of the flesh, leaving about $\frac{1}{8}$ inch. Err on the side of a little too much potato flesh, if you must. Reserve the removed potato flesh for another use.

5. Lightly brush the melted butter on the outside of the potato skins and drizzle the rest inside the potatoes. Season to taste with salt and pepper. Transfer the potato skins to a baking sheet and bake for 10 to 15 minutes, or until crisp and lightly browned. Garnish with parsley.

HERBED NEW POTATOES

This delicious and simple potato dish is always welcome at the table. Make it with the firmest, freshest new potatoes you can find, and cook them carefully. We peel a strip of the red skin around the middle of the potato for aesthetic reasons; you don't have to do this if you find it too fancy. You can also use small white-skinned potatoes if you can't find red ones.

SERVES 6

$1\frac{1}{2}$ **to 2 pounds small red new potatoes**
1 tablespoon salt
$\frac{1}{4}$ cup Clarified Butter (page 231) **or olive oil**
2 tablespoons chopped fresh rosemary
2 tablespoons chopped fresh curly-leaf parsley

1. Wash the potatoes under cold water. Peel a 1-inch strip around the center of each potato.

2. Put the potatoes in a large pot and add enough cold water to cover by 1 inch. Add the salt and set the pot over high heat. Bring to a boil and cook for 10 to 12 minutes, or until a skewer inserted in a potato easily pierces the skin, but the center is still firm.

3. Meanwhile, preheat the oven to 450°F.

4. Drain the potatoes and transfer to a baking sheet. Drizzle with the butter or oil and toss gently to coat. Sprinkle the rosemary over the potatoes and roast for 30 to 35 minutes, or until the potatoes are cooked through and nicely browned. Shake the pan or stir the potatoes every 10 minutes during roasting.

5. Sprinkle the parsley over the hot potatoes, shake the pan to coat evenly with parsley and the butter still in the pan, and serve hot.

MASHED POTATOES

These are so good because they are so easy to make. Potatoes, butter, heavy cream, sour cream, and salt and pepper. What can go wrong? For garlic mashed potatoes, use Garlic Butter (page 224) in place of the plain unsalted butter.

SERVES 6

5 pounds russet or all-purpose potatoes, peeled
1 cup (2 sticks) **unsalted butter**
1 cup heavy cream
1 cup sour cream
1 tablespoon salt
1 teaspoon freshly ground white pepper

1. Cut the potatoes into approximate 1½-inch cubes and transfer to a large pot. Add enough cold water to cover the potatoes by 1 inch and bring to a boil over high heat. Reduce the heat to medium and simmer for 20 to 25 minutes, or until the potatoes are fork-tender. Be careful not to overcook. Immediately drain in a colander.

2. Meanwhile, in a saucepan, combine the butter and cream over medium heat, and cook until the butter melts. Do not boil. Set aside.

3. Transfer the drained potatoes to the bowl of an electric mixer fitted with the paddle attachment and mix on low speed for 2 to 3 minutes, or until the potatoes start to break up and blend together. You may have to do this in batches. Gradually add the sour cream and mix until combined. Season with salt and pepper. (Alternatively, mash the potatoes by hand with a potato masher.)

4. With the mixer still on low speed, slowly add the hot cream-butter mixture. When all is added, increase the speed to medium and mix for 30 to 40 seconds, or until thoroughly mixed. Add more warm cream if necessary for the correct consistency. The potatoes should not be completely smooth.

LYONNAISE POTATOES

This is a tasty way to use up leftover potatoes, although Lyonnaise Potatoes are good enough to bake the potatoes expressly to make the dish. You may turn away when you see that this calls for a cup of bacon fat, but the fat really adds to the flavor in a way that neither olive oil nor butter would. When we tested the recipe for this book we tried it several different ways and decided the bacon fat was integral. You don't have to make these too often, but when you do, definitely use bacon fat. The dish has been on our menu for years—and I see no reason to take it off. Ever!

SERVES 6

3¾ pounds baking potatoes, baked and cooled
    (3 to 5 large baking potatoes; see Note)
1 cup bacon fat (see Note)
2¼ pounds Spanish onions (3 medium onions)**, sliced ¼ inch thick**
Salt and freshly ground white pepper
1 teaspoon chopped fresh curly-leaf parsley

1. Cut the ends off the potatoes, peel, and slice in half lengthwise. Cut each half across into ⅜-inch-thick slices and set aside.

2. Heat a large sauté pan over medium-high heat. When warm, add half the bacon fat and heat until hot. Add half the potatoes and toss. Cook for 4 to 5 minutes, or until light golden brown.

3. Add half the onions, season to taste with salt and pepper, and sauté for 8 to 10 minutes, or until golden brown. Remove to a large bowl, cover loosely, and set aside to keep warm. Repeat to make the second batch with the remaining fat, potatoes, onions, and seasoning.

4. When all the potatoes are in the bowl, add the parsley and toss. Serve immediately.

Note: For 1 cup of bacon fat, cook 1½ pounds of bacon until crisp. Reserve the bacon for another use. To bake potatoes, scrub the skins, pierce them several times with the tines of a fork, and bake them for 1 hour to 1 hour and 20 minutes in a preheated 400°F. oven until tender when pierced with a small knife or skewer.

8

DESSERTS

Chocolate Velvet Cake

Morton's Legendary Hot Chocolate Cake

Chocolate Soufflé

Lemon Soufflé

Key Lime Pie

Cold Grand Marnier Soufflé

Upside-Down Apple Pie

Custard with Raspberries

CHOCOLATE VELVET CAKE

This is the ideal chocolate cake for a large party. It is very rich, so you can cut slender slices to make the cake go further. It must be made well ahead of time, so it's ready when you want to serve it. You will need a 10-inch springform pan, but otherwise you probably have all the equipment you'll need, particularly if you like to bake. Use the best dark chocolate (a general term for bittersweet and semisweet chocolate) you can find for this. You won't be sorry.

SERVES 10 TO 12; MAKES 1 CAKE

CAKE
- **3 tablespoons unsalted butter, plus more for greasing the pan**
- **2 tablespoons unsweetened cocoa powder**
- **$\frac{1}{4}$ teaspoon pure vanilla extract**
- **5 large eggs**
- **7 tablespoons sugar**
- **5 tablespoons plus 1 teaspoon all-purpose flour**

FILLING AND TOPPING
- **$1\frac{2}{3}$ pounds semisweet or bittersweet chocolate**
- **3 large eggs, separated**
- **1 tablespoon instant coffee granules**
- **$\frac{1}{3}$ cup praline paste**
- **$\frac{1}{4}$ cup (2 ounces) dark crème de cacao**
- **$\frac{1}{4}$ cup (2 ounces) dark rum**
- **$\frac{1}{4}$ cup (2 ounces) Kirsch**
- **2 cups heavy cream**
- **2 tablespoons plus 2 teaspoons sugar**
- **1 tablespoon unsalted butter**

recipe continues

1. Preheat the oven to 350°F. Butter and flour a 9-inch round cake pan that is 2 inches deep. Set aside.

2. To prepare the cake, in a small saucepan, melt the 3 tablespoons butter over low heat and set aside, covered, to keep warm.

3. In another small saucepan, bring ¼ cup of water to a boil over medium-high heat. Whisk in the cocoa powder and vanilla until smooth and set aside.

4. In the top of a double boiler, combine the eggs and sugar and set over simmering water over medium heat. Whisk continuously for about 3 minutes, or until frothy and a deep golden yellow. The mixture will be hot to the touch (about 105°F.).

5. Transfer the egg mixture to the bowl of an electric mixer fitted with the whisk attachment. Beat on high speed for about 5 minutes, or until light and fluffy.

6. Fold 1 cup of the egg mixture into the cocoa.

7. Sift the flour over the egg mixture still in the bowl of the electric mixer and gently fold into the batter. Fold the cocoa mixture into the batter. Fold the warm butter into the batter just until mixed. Do not overmix.

8. Pour the batter into the prepared pan and smooth the surface. Bake for 30 to 35 minutes, or until the cake begins to pull away from the sides of the pan and a toothpick inserted in the center comes out clean.

9. Let the cake cool in the pan for about 5 minutes, then invert the cake onto a wire rack to cool completely. When the cake is cool, slice it in half horizontally using a serrated knife. Line a 9-inch springform pan with plastic wrap so that the ends of the plastic wrap extend over the side of the pan. Put the better-looking half of the cake in the springform pan. Reserve the other half for another use. (Wrapped well in plastic, it will keep in the freezer for up to 1 month.) Set the pan aside.

10. To prepare the filling, chop 1⅓ pounds of the chocolate into small chunks. Put the chocolate in the top of a double boiler set over gently simmering water over medium heat. Slowly melt the chocolate. Set aside. (Reserve the remaining ⅓ pound of chocolate for the topping.)

11. Put the egg yolks in the top of a double boiler set over simmering water over medium heat and whisk vigorously for about 1 minute, or until warm to the touch. Take care that the eggs do not cook. Remove the top of the double boiler from the heat and whisk in the coffee granules and then the praline paste, crème de cacao, rum, and Kirsch. Whisk in the melted chocolate and set aside.

12. In the bowl of an electric mixer fitted with the whisk attachment, whip $1\frac{1}{4}$ cups of the cream on high for $1\frac{1}{2}$ to 2 minutes, or until soft peaks form. Set aside while you beat the egg whites.

13. In the clean, dry bowl of an electric mixer fitted with the whisk attachment (make sure the whisk is clean and dry), whisk the egg whites for 1 to 2 minutes, or until soft peaks form. Add the sugar to the meringue and whisk for 90 seconds longer, or until the egg whites form stiff peaks.

14. Fold the chocolate mixture into the whipped cream, and then fold this chocolate-cream mixture into the meringue.

15. To assemble the cake, pour the filling on top of the cake layer. It should fill the pan about three-quarters full. Gently tap the pan on the countertop to remove any air bubbles, and smooth with a spatula. Cover the cake with plastic wrap and refrigerate for at least 8 hours, or until the filling is set.

16. Finely chop the remaining $\frac{1}{3}$ pound of chocolate. In the top of a double boiler set over gently simmering water set over medium heat, combine the chopped chocolate, butter, and remaining $\frac{3}{4}$ cup of cream. Whisk until the chocolate melts and the mixture is smooth. Set aside for about 10 minutes to cool until warm.

17. Remove the cake from the springform pan by releasing the sides. (The plastic wrap will help remove it, too.) Using a wide spatula, carefully transfer the cake, still on the metal base of the pan, to a wire rack set on a baking sheet or pan. Ladle the chocolate topping over the cake and spread it over the cake so that the sides and top are evenly and completely covered. Refrigerate the cake for about 15 minutes, or until the topping is set.

18. Carefully transfer the cake to a serving plate or platter. If you can remove it from the metal base, do so. Otherwise, leave it in place. Let the cake sit at room temperature for 15 or 20 minutes before slicing.

MORTON'S LEGENDARY HOT CHOCOLATE CAKE

This is our number one dessert, followed by soufflés. If you like molten chocolate cakes, you'll be thrilled at how easy they are to make. To get the right consistency, though, you must bake small, individual cakes; for these, you will need 6-ounce soufflé dishes or ramekins.

SERVES 6

1½ cups unsalted butter, at room temperature,
    plus more for the soufflé cups
Granulated sugar
12 ounces bittersweet or semisweet chocolate,
    coarsely chopped
8 large egg yolks, plus 7 large eggs
1½ cups confectioners' sugar
¾ cup all-purpose flour
18 fresh raspberries
6 scoops vanilla ice cream

1. Preheat the oven to 350°F. Generously butter six 6-ounce soufflé cups and sprinkle each with granulated sugar. Tap out the excess sugar.

2. In the top of a double boiler set over barely simmering water, melt the butter and chocolate together. Remove the top of the double boiler pan from the heat.

3. In the bowl of an electric mixer fitted with the whisk attachment and set on low speed, beat the egg yolks and eggs for about 2 minutes, or until light and smooth. With the mixer running, pour the melted chocolate into the bowl and mix for about 2 minutes longer.

4. Put the confectioners' sugar and flour in a fine-mesh sieve and sprinkle into the chocolate mixture. With the mixer on medium speed, beat for 30 seconds, or until well mixed.

5. Pour the batter into the prepared soufflé cups, leaving about ¼ inch of space below the rim. Set the soufflé cups on a baking sheet and bake for 18 to 20 minutes, or until puffed and about 1 inch higher than the rim. The centers will be soft but not sticky.

6. Remove the cakes from the oven and immediately invert each onto a serving plate. Remove the cup and garnish each plate with three raspberries and a scoop of vanilla ice cream.

CHOCOLATE SOUFFLÉ

Chocolate soufflé has been on our menu since we opened the first Morton's Steakhouse. We make our soufflés in 3½-cup soufflé dishes, which are big enough for two servings.

SERVES 4

3 tablespoons unsweetened cocoa powder
1 tablespoon all-purpose flour
2 teaspoons cornstarch
1 cup cold whole milk
4 large egg yolks, plus 8 large egg whites (1¼ cups),
   at room temperature
½ cup granulated sugar, plus additional
   for the soufflé dishes
2 teaspoons unsalted butter, at room temperature
Confectioners' sugar, for dusting
2 tablespoons finely chopped bittersweet or
   semisweet chocolate (1 ounce)
Sabayon Sauce (page 197)

1. In a small bowl, whisk together the cocoa powder, flour, and cornstarch. Stir in ⅓ cup of the milk and mix well. Set aside.

2. In a medium saucepan, heat the remaining ⅔ cup milk over medium heat until steaming hot but not boiling. Cover and set aside.

3. Meanwhile, in the top of a double boiler over gently simmering water, whisk the egg yolks and 2 tablespoons of the granulated sugar for about 2 minutes, or until the sugar dissolves and the mixture is deep golden yellow and foamy. (The temperature should be between 105° and 110°F.)

4. Add the hot milk, alternating it with the cocoa mixture. Whisk just to blend and then return the mixture to the saucepan that held the milk. Over low heat, cook the mixture for $1^1/2$ to 2 minutes, whisking vigorously, until smooth and thick.

5. Remove the pan from the heat. Using a handheld mixer (you may do this in a standing mixer if you don't have a handheld mixer), beat for 2 minutes. Add the butter, $1/2$ teaspoon at a time. Blend the pudding well after each addition. Scrape the pudding into a mixing bowl. Generously dust the surface with confectioners' sugar. Cover loosely and set aside for 30 minutes.

6. Preheat the oven to 375°F. Put the oven rack in the lowest position.

7. Generously butter two $3^1/2$-cup soufflé dishes and sprinkle each dish with 2 teaspoons of granulated sugar, taking care to coat the sides and bottoms completely.

8. In the bowl of an electric mixer fitted with the whisk attachment and set on high speed, whisk the egg whites for 30 seconds until foamy. Slowly add the remaining 6 tablespoons of granulated sugar and whisk for about 90 seconds, or until the egg whites form semi-stiff peaks and appear glossy and tender. Do not over-mix the egg whites; they should not be grainy or dry looking or the soufflés may not rise properly.

9. Stir the chopped chocolate into the pudding. Using a rubber spatula, fold one-third of the egg whites into the pudding until well blended. Use the rubber spatula to scrape this mixture back into the bowl containing the whites. Gently fold the pudding and whites together until mixed and no white spots remain. Once this happens, stop folding so that you won't deflate the whites. From this point onward, work steadily. Do not rush but do not stop until the soufflés are in the oven.

recipe continues

10. Divide the soufflé mixture between the dishes, filling each about three-quarters full. With the rubber spatula, form a peak in the center of each soufflé. Transfer the soufflé dishes to a baking pan large enough to hold them (we use one that measures 9×13 inches). Pour in enough hot water to come two-thirds of the way up the sides of the soufflé dishes.

11. Carefully transfer the baking pan to the oven. Bake for 28 to 30 minutes, or until the soufflés rise about 2 inches above the rim and the surface is darkened.

12. Carefully remove the soufflé dishes from the water bath. Dust each with confectioners' sugar. Serve the Sabayon Sauce on the side.

LEMON SOUFFLÉ

Soufflés are like Rolls-Royces or fine champagne: classy. We love the drama as they are carried through the restaurant. Morton's has always had lemon, Grand Marnier, and chocolate soufflés on the menu, and we added the raspberry soufflé later. All are delicious and surprisingly easy to make. Be sure to beat the egg whites until glossy, and mix them into the soufflé pudding with a sure but gentle hand. Once the soufflés are in the oven, don't open the oven door. You will be rewarded with a glorious dessert!

SERVES 4

1 tablespoon all-purpose flour
1 tablespoon cornstarch
1 cup cold whole milk
4 large egg yolks, plus 8 large egg whites (1¼ cups), at room temperature
½ cup granulated sugar, plus additional for the soufflé dishes
¾ teaspoon pure vanilla extract
4 teaspoons unsalted butter, at room temperature
2 tablespoons finely grated lemon zest, plus additional for garnish
1 tablespoon fresh lemon juice
Confectioners' sugar, for dusting
Sabayon Sauce (recipe follows)

1. In a small bowl, whisk together the flour and cornstarch. Stir in 2 tablespoons of the milk and mix well. Set aside.

2. In a medium saucepan, heat the remaining milk over medium heat until steaming hot but not boiling. Cover and set aside.

3. Meanwhile, in the top of a double boiler over gently simmering water, whisk the egg yolks, 2 tablespoons of the granulated sugar, and the vanilla for about 2 minutes, or until the sugar dissolves and the mixture is deep golden yellow and foamy. (The temperature should be between 105° and 110°F.)

4. Add the hot milk, alternating it with the cornstarch-flour mixture. Whisk just to blend and then return the mixture to the saucepan that held the milk. Over low heat, cook the mixture for $1\frac{1}{2}$ to 2 minutes, whisking vigorously, until smooth and thick.

5. Remove the pan from the heat. Using a handheld mixer (you may do this in a standing mixer if you don't have a handheld mixer), beat for 2 minutes. Add 2 teaspoons of the butter, $\frac{1}{2}$ teaspoon at a time. Blend well after each addition. Add the lemon zest and juice and blend well. Scrape the pudding into a mixing bowl. Generously dust the surface with confectioners' sugar. Cover loosely and set aside for 30 minutes.

6. Preheat the oven to 375°F. Put the oven rack in the lowest position.

7. Generously butter two $3\frac{1}{2}$-cup soufflé dishes with the remaining 2 teaspoons of butter. Sprinkle each dish with 2 teaspoons of granulated sugar, taking care to coat the sides and bottoms completely.

8. In the bowl of an electric mixer fitted with the whisk attachment and set on high speed, whisk the egg whites for 30 seconds until foamy. Slowly add the remaining 6 tablespoons of granulated sugar and whisk for about 90 seconds, or until the egg whites form semi-stiff peaks and appear glossy and tender. Do not overmix the egg whites; they should not be grainy or dry looking or the soufflés may not rise properly.

9. Stir the lemon pudding. Using a rubber spatula, fold one-third of the egg whites into the pudding until well blended. Use the rubber spatula to scrape this mixture back into the bowl containing the whites. Gently fold the pudding and whites together until mixed and no white spots remain. Once this happens, stop folding so that you won't deflate the whites. From this point onward, work steadily. Do not rush but do not stop until the soufflés are in the oven.

recipe continues

10. Divide the soufflé mixture between the dishes, filling each about three-quarters full. With the rubber spatula, form a peak in the center of each soufflé. Transfer the soufflé dishes to a baking pan large enough to hold them (we use one that measures 9×13 inches). Pour in enough hot water to come two-thirds of the way up the sides of the soufflé dishes.

11. Carefully transfer the baking pan to the oven. Bake for about 25 minutes, or until the soufflés rise about 2 inches above the rim and the surface is golden brown.

12. Carefully remove the soufflé dishes from the water bath. Dust each with confectioners' sugar and garnish with lemon zest. Serve the Sabayon Sauce on the side.

VARIATIONS
RASPBERRY SOUFFLÉ
Add 1 tablespoon of raspberry liqueur, such as Chambord, and 1 tablespoon of puréed and strained frozen raspberries to the pudding in step 5 when you scrape the pudding into the bowl. Mix well and then dust the surface of the pudding with confectioners' sugar, as instructed in the recipe. Garnish each soufflé with three fresh raspberries.

GRAND MARNIER SOUFFLÉ
Add 2 tablespoons of finely grated orange zest and 2 tablespoons of Grand Marnier liqueur to the pudding in step 5 when you scrape the pudding into the bowl. Mix well and then dust the surface of the pudding with confectioners' sugar, as instructed in the recipe. Use more orange zest to garnish the soufflés.

SABAYON SAUCE

This sweet, creamy sauce complements soufflés perfectly. You can make it ahead of time—even a few days ahead if that suits you—so that you aren't rushing around the kitchen when the soufflés are ready to serve. Its staying power contributes to its texture, which is thicker and fluffier than classic sabayon sauce. It's delicious served with berries, fruit pies, and pound cake, too.

MAKES 2 GENEROUS CUPS

3 large egg yolks

2 tablespoons marsala wine

2 tablespoons sugar

$\frac{1}{3}$ cup whipped topping (see Note)

$\frac{1}{3}$ cup heavy cream

1. In the top of a double boiler set over simmering water over medium heat, stir together the egg yolks, wine, and sugar. Whisk for about 2 minutes, or until the sabayon is a light amber color and slightly thickened and foamy. Set aside to cool to room temperature.

2. Put the whipped topping in a bowl. Using a handheld electric mixer set on high speed, whisk the topping for $2\frac{1}{2}$ minutes, or until it forms very stiff peaks. Transfer to a mixing bowl. You will have about $1\frac{1}{4}$ cups of whipped topping.

3. In the bowl of an electric mixer fitted with the wire whisk and set on high, whip the cream for about 1 minute, until stiff peaks form. Fold the cream into the whipped topping.

4. Whisk the cooled sabayon base again and then fold into the cream mixture. Serve immediately or refrigerate in a tightly covered container for up to 2 days.

NOTE: We use Rich's Whip Topping, which is sold in the frozen-food sections of some supermarkets alongside the whipped dessert toppings. It stabilizes the sauce. If you can't find Rich's Whip Topping, use Cool Whip instead. The texture may not be quite the same, but it will be good.

KEY LIME PIE

The first thing you will notice about this pie is that we don't use Key lime juice but instead rely on bottled lime juice or juice squeezed from any type of lime. You could quibble that this is not an official Key lime pie, but it's a name everyone recognizes and no one has ever been disappointed by the pie. It's one of the easiest of all our desserts to make and also one of the best.

SERVES 6 TO 8; MAKES ONE 10-INCH PIE

One 10-inch prepared graham cracker pie crust (see Note)
1 large egg white, plus 15 large egg yolks
Two 14-ounce cans sweetened condensed milk, such as Eagle Brand
1 cup plus 1 tablespoon lime juice (see Note)
6 tablespoons sugar
Sweetened Whipped Cream (recipe follows),
    for garnish

1. Preheat the oven to 375°F.

2. Brush the inside bottom and sides of the pie crust with the egg white (you may not need all of it) and bake for 5 minutes to set. Let cool on a wire rack.

3. In the bowl of an electric mixer fitted with the paddle attachment and set on medium speed, mix the egg yolks, condensed milk, lime juice, and sugar for about 2 minutes, or until the sugar has dissolved and the mixture is smooth. Scrape the bowl from the bottom during mixing to make sure everything gets combined.

4. Set the pie shell on a baking sheet. Pour the filling into the pie shell so that it reaches the rim. Bake for 30 to 35 minutes, or until just firm in the center and the filling is golden brown around the edges. Remove the pie from the oven and refrigerate immediately for at least 3 hours or overnight.

5. Serve the pie garnished with whipped cream.

Notes: At the restaurant, we usually use Keebler Redi-Crust, but you could use another brand or even make your own.

We use RealLime lime juice, but another brand would work well, too. You could also squeeze fresh limes for the juice; you'll need 10 to 12 of them.

SWEETENED WHIPPED CREAM

You'll find numerous uses for this. Begin with good heavy cream (sometimes labeled whipping cream), and if you prefer it less sweet, reduce the amount of sugar by a few teaspoons. Make sure everything is cold before you begin: the cream, the bowl, and the whisk. We tell our cooks that the cream is correctly whipped when the whip can stand on its own in the bowl.

MAKES 4 GENEROUS CUPS

1 pint cold heavy cream
2½ tablespoons confectioners' sugar

1. In the chilled bowl of an electric mixer fitted with a chilled whisk attachment and set on medium-high speed, whip the cream for about 1 minute, or until thickened.

2. Add the sugar and whip until incorporated and the cream forms soft peaks. Whip longer if you want firmer peaks, but take care not to overmix. Use immediately or refrigerate for up to 1 hour.

COLD GRAND MARNIER SOUFFLÉ

A chilled soufflé is not really a soufflé but a chilled dessert lightened with whipped cream and stabilized with gelatin. There's nothing tricky about this one. It's like eating a cold, sweet cloud.

SERVES 6

$1\frac{1}{2}$ **cups whipping cream**
4 large eggs, plus 3 large egg yolks
$\frac{1}{2}$ **cup sugar**
Two $\frac{1}{4}$-ounce packets unflavored gelatin powder
   ($1\frac{1}{2}$ tablespoons)
$\frac{1}{4}$ **cup Grand Marnier or other orange-flavored liqueur**
Store-bought melba sauce or raspberry purée
1 tablespoon finely grated orange zest
6 raspberries
6 mint leaves

1. In the bowl of an electric mixer fitted with the whisk attachment, whip the cream until it forms stiff peaks. Set aside.

2. In the top of a double boiler set over simmering water, whisk the eggs, egg yolks, and sugar for about 2 minutes, or until warm to the touch (about 105°F.), golden yellow, and frothy. Transfer the egg mixture to the bowl of an electric mixer fitted with the whisk attachment or remove the top of the double boiler and use a handheld mixer or immersion blender. Whisk for about 3 minutes, or until cool. Wrap your hands around the outside of the bowl to determine when the mixture cools.

3. Meanwhile, in a small bowl, sprinkle the gelatin over ¼ cup of warm water to dissolve. Add the Grand Marnier and dissolved gelatin to the cooled egg mixture and beat on medium-low until the liquid is incorporated.

4. Using a rubber spatula, fold the egg mixture into the whipped cream just until combined. Do not over-mix. You will have more than 6 cups of batter.

5. Divide the mixture among six 8-ounce soufflé dishes. Refrigerate for at least 2 hours until chilled. The soufflés can be refrigerated for up to 24 hours.

6. To serve, remove the soufflés from the dishes by running a blunt kitchen knife around the inside of the dishes. Put a chilled dessert plate on top of each soufflé, and holding the dish and plate securely, invert. Gently shake the dish as you lift it off the soufflé.

7. Garnish each plate with a drizzle of melba sauce, orange zest, a raspberry, and a mint leaf.

UPSIDE-DOWN APPLE PIE

I love a good apple pie. There's nothing inherently American about them, despite the popular expression; I grew up in Germany eating apple desserts. Take my word for it, this is one of the best I have ever tasted. It's a little different from traditional apple pie: we make them in individual servings and top the apples with a cake-like batter.

SERVES 6

APPLE PIE FILLING

$1\frac{1}{4}$ cups golden raisins ($7\frac{1}{2}$ ounces)

$\frac{2}{3}$ cup Grand Marnier or other orange-flavored liqueur

1 lemon

7 to 8 Granny Smith apples ($2\frac{3}{4}$ to 3 pounds)

5 tablespoons unsalted butter

$\frac{2}{3}$ cup granulated sugar

$\frac{3}{4}$ teaspoon ground cinnamon

$\frac{1}{8}$ teaspoon freshly grated nutmeg

1 tablespoon cornstarch

APPLE PIE BATTER

1 cup granulated sugar

$6\frac{1}{2}$ tablespoons unsalted butter, softened

2 large eggs

1 teaspoon pure vanilla extract

2 cups all-purpose flour

$\frac{1}{2}$ teaspoon baking powder

$\frac{1}{2}$ teaspoon baking soda

$\frac{1}{2}$ teaspoon salt

$\frac{3}{4}$ cup buttermilk

Granulated brown sugar or raw sugar, such as Sugar in the Raw, for dusting the soufflé dishes

Vanilla ice cream, for serving

6 mint sprigs, for garnish

recipe continues

1. To make the filling, in a small saucepan, combine the raisins and orange liqueur and bring to a simmer over medium-low heat. Simmer gently for 5 to 7 minutes, or until the liquid has evaporated. Set aside.

2. Fill a large nonreactive bowl with water and squeeze the lemon juice into the water to make acidulated water.

3. Peel, core, and halve the apples. Cut the halves into $\frac{1}{4}$-inch-thick slices. You will have about 12 cups of sliced apples. Submerge the apple slices in the acidulated water.

4. In a large skillet, melt half the butter over medium heat. As soon as the butter melts, stir in half of the granulated sugar, half of the cinnamon, and half of the nutmeg. When the sugar is moistened, add about half of the raisins, toss to coat, and cook for 2 to 3 minutes, or until the raisins are heated through. Drain half of the apples, add to the raisin mixture, and increase the heat to medium-high. Cook, stirring often, for about 8 minutes, or until the apples are limp and release their juices, and the liquid is syrupy. Transfer to a bowl and cover to keep warm.

5. Repeat with the remaining butter, sugar, cinnamon, nutmeg, raisins, and apples. When the second batch is done, return the first batch of apples to the pan. You will have about $6\frac{1}{2}$ cups of apples.

6. In a small dish, stir the cornstarch with 1 tablespoon of water. Add to the skillet and cook, tossing the apples, for about 1 minute, or until the sauce thickens and looks glossy. Remove from the heat and set aside to cool to room temperature. (The filling may be made to this point and refrigerated for up to 3 days. Bring to room temperature before using.)

7. To prepare the batter, in the bowl of an electric mixer fitted with the paddle attachment set on medium-high speed, beat the granulated sugar and butter for about 2 minutes, or until well blended. Add the eggs and vanilla and beat until well mixed.

8. In a mixing bowl, whisk together the flour, baking powder, baking soda, and salt until well mixed.

9. With the electric mixer on medium-low, add a third of the flour mixture to the batter and mix for about 2 minutes, or until well combined. Add half of the buttermilk and mix for about 1 minute, or until well combined. Add the next third of the flour mixture and mix until thoroughly incorporated. Finally, mix in the rest of the buttermilk, followed by the final third of the flour. Mix for 2 minutes, scraping down the sides of the bowl with a rubber spatula, or until incorporated. You will have about $3\frac{1}{3}$ cups of batter.

10. Preheat the oven to 350°F. Position the oven rack in the center of the oven.

11. To assemble the pies, brush the inside of each of six 8-ounce soufflé dishes with butter. Coat the inside of the dishes with brown sugar. Fill each dish with a cup of the filling, until a little more than three-quarters full. Top with the batter, dividing it evenly among the dishes. Depending on the amount of apples in each ramekin, you may have $\frac{1}{3}$ to $\frac{1}{2}$ cup of batter left over. Use a rubber spatula to smooth the top of the batter so that it is level with the lip of the dish. Run a finger around the edge of each dish to level them. Let the filling settle for a few minutes and add more if necessary to fill the ramekins.

12. Put the dishes on a baking sheet and bake for about 30 minutes, or until the top crust is golden brown. Let the pies rest on wire cooling racks for at least 10 minutes and not longer than 20 minutes. Put a dessert plate on top of each of the soufflé dishes and, holding the dish and plate securely, invert. Gently lift the dish off the pie.

13. To serve, put a scoop of ice cream next to each pie and garnish each plate with a mint sprig.

CUSTARD WITH RASPBERRIES

This is similar to a crème caramel, and is absolutely luscious. Few things satisfy the soul like a good custard. And when that custard is topped with a dripping crown of caramel and garnished with raspberries or strawberries, it's a dessert sent from heaven.

SERVES 10

3$\frac{1}{2}$ **cups sugar**
7 large eggs, plus 4 large egg yolks
8 cups whole milk
1 teaspoon pure vanilla extract
1$\frac{1}{4}$ **pints raspberries** (or strawberries)
10 mint leaves

1. Preheat the oven to 325°F.

2. In a small, heavy saucepan over low heat, melt 2 cups of the sugar, stirring frequently with a wooden spoon. As soon as the sugar starts to melt, stir continuously for about 15 minutes, or until it turns golden brown. Be careful; the sugar gets very hot.

3. Carefully pour enough melted sugar into each of ten 8-ounce custard cups to cover the bottom. Quickly swirl the cups so that the sugar covers them completely. Put the custard cups in a roasting pan large enough to hold them without touching and set aside.

4. In a large mixing bowl, whisk together the eggs and yolks.

5. In a medium saucepan, heat the milk over medium-high heat. When the milk is hot, add the remaining 1$\frac{1}{2}$ cups of sugar and the vanilla and cook, stirring, just until the milk starts to steam and the sugar dissolves. Reduce the heat as necessary to keep the milk from bubbling.

6. Very slowly add $\frac{1}{2}$ cup of the hot milk to the eggs, whisking constantly, to temper the eggs. Slowly add the rest of the milk, whisking gently, until smooth. Skim off any bubbles that appear on the surface.

7. Divide the custard evenly among the prepared custard cups. Pop any bubbles on the surface of the custard.

8. Set the roasting pan on the oven rack, pulled part of the way out of the oven. Pour enough hot water into the pan to come about three-quarters of the way up the sides of the custard cups. Carefully slide the rack back into the oven and bake for 40 to 45 minutes, or until the custards are set, still jiggle in the center, and are very lightly browned around the edges. Remove the custard cups from the pan and transfer to a baking sheet to cool slightly. Refrigerate to cool completely.

9. To serve, remove the custards from the refrigerator. Run a small, blunt knife around the inside of the cups. Put a chilled dessert plate on top of each cup, and holding the cup and plate securely, invert. Gently shake the cup as you lift it off the custard. Let any excess caramel run onto the plate. Garnish the plate with some raspberries and a mint leaf.

CELEBRITY CLIP

Russell Crowe and Renée Zellweger turned the Toronto Morton's into a second home while filming **Cinderella Man**. Both had access to a private entrance so that they could come and go as they pleased and both seemed to appreciate the atmosphere and discreet service. One night Crowe brought the entire film crew for dinner and another night, he bought a round of drinks for a group of Toronto Maple Leaf players sitting at a nearby table. This turned out to be a good move for the movie star, who then spent the evening exuberantly talking hockey with the players!

BÉARNAISE SAUCE

WHIPPED HORSERADISH

SAUCE BORDELAISE

9

SAUCES, DRESSINGS, AND CONDIMENTS

Au Jus

Sauce Bordelaise

Hollandaise Sauce

Béarnaise Sauce

Cream Sauce

Beurre Blanc

Whipped Horseradish

Apricot Chutney

Diablo Sauce

Mustard-Mayonnaise Sauce

Garlic Butter

Cocktail Sauce

Classic Vinaigrette

Dijon Vinaigrette

Morton's Blue Cheese Dressing

Caesar Dressing

Clarified Butter

Alex's Bread Crumbs

AU JUS

In every recipe for steak, as well as some others, we suggest you spoon some Au Jus over the meat before serving. You may decide to forgo this step, relying instead on the natural juices in the meat. But if you make this sauce, your steaks will have just a little more flavor and a little more flair. It keeps in the refrigerator for a few days, so you can make it ahead of time.

MAKES ABOUT 1 GENEROUS CUP

1 cup store-bought veal demi-glace (see Note, page 111)
2½ teaspoons commercial beef base (see Note)
1¼ teaspoons commercial chicken base (see Note)
½ teaspoon whole black peppercorns
⅛ teaspoon garlic powder
⅛ teaspoon dried thyme
1 bay leaf
Pinch of freshly ground white pepper

1. In a medium saucepan, combine 1¼ cups of water with the demi-glace, beef base, chicken base, peppercorns, garlic powder, thyme, bay leaf, and ground pepper. Whisk well. Bring to a boil over medium-high heat and cook at a boil, uncovered, whisking occasionally, for about 25 minutes, or until glossy and smooth.

2. Strain through a chinois or a fine-mesh sieve into a metal bowl. Discard the solids. Let cool, then cover and refrigerate for at least 1 hour until chilled. Scrape any fat that has congealed on the surface. Use right away or transfer to a lidded container and refrigerate for up to 3 days.

Notes: If you decide to double or triple the amount of Au Jus you make at one time, cool the strained sauce in a bowl set in a larger one filled with ice cubes and water. This is the best way to cool large amounts of hot liquid. For the 1 cup we make here, it's not necessary.

You can buy beef and chicken bases in local supermarkets or search for them online. We use beef and chicken bases from Bear Creek Gourmet Kitchens. Another good brand is Superior Touch Better Than Bouillon. These pastelike products are sold in small jars. They are intensely flavored, so measure carefully.

SAUCE BORDELAISE

MAKES ABOUT 2½ CUPS

1 cup undiluted store-bought veal demi-glace
   (see Note, page 111)
1 tablespoon Clarified Butter (page 231)
¼ cup chopped shallots
2 tablespoons chopped garlic
1 tablespoon black peppercorns
3 to 4 thyme sprigs
2 cups dry red wine
Salt and freshly ground black pepper
1 tablespoon unsalted butter

1. In a medium saucepan, combine the demi-glace and 2½ cups of water over medium heat and bring to a boil. Reduce the heat and simmer for about 15 minutes, or until slightly reduced. Set aside.

2. Meanwhile, in a large saucepan, heat the Clarified Butter over medium heat. Add the shallots, garlic, peppercorns, and thyme and sauté for about 5 minutes, or until the shallots and garlic have softened without browning.

3. Add the red wine to the saucepan, bring to a simmer, and cook for about 15 minutes, or until reduced to a syrup.

4. Add the demi-glace mixture to the wine-shallot mixture and simmer for 15 to 20 minutes, or until the flavors blend and the sauce is thick enough to coat a spoon.

5. Strain the sauce through a fine-mesh sieve into a small saucepan. Season to taste with salt and pepper, if necessary. Whisk the tablespoon of butter into the sauce over low heat to give it shine. Take care that the sauce does not boil.

HOLLANDAISE SAUCE

Hollandaise is a lovely, rich, slightly tangy sauce that complements beef as well as vegetables such as asparagus and artichokes. While it's not an everyday accompaniment, it can be the pièce de résistance of a special meal. Some home cooks fear making hollandaise because it has the tendency to break (curdle). Our method is as close to foolproof as you can get. Make the sauce shortly before serving; it does not hold well.

MAKES ABOUT 2 CUPS

5 large egg yolks
1½ cups Clarified Butter (page 231)
1½ teaspoons fresh lemon juice
⅛ teaspoon Worcestershire sauce
Dash of Tabasco or other hot pepper sauce
¼ teaspoon salt
⅛ teaspoon freshly ground white pepper

1. In the bottom half of a double boiler, bring about 2 inches of water to a boil over high heat. The water should not touch the bottom of the top portion of the double boiler. Reduce the heat to medium so that the water is simmering.

2. Put the egg yolks and 2 tablespoons of water in the top of the double boiler and set over the simmering water. Whisk the eggs continuously for 2 to 2½ minutes, or until the eggs are thick and foamy and their color lightens. Watch the eggs carefully; they must not scramble and cook. Remove the top of the double boiler from the heat.

3. In a small saucepan, heat the butter over medium-low heat. Very gradually add half of the warm butter to the eggs, whisking constantly. Add 1 tablespoon of water and continue to whisk as you add the rest of the melted butter and the sauce emulsifies.

4. Stir in the lemon juice, Worcestershire and Tabasco sauces, salt, and pepper. Return the top of the double boiler to the heat over the simmering water (add more water to the bottom of the double boiler if necessary). Cook gently until the sauce registers 110° to 120°F. on an instant-read thermometer. Serve warm.

BÉARNAISE SAUCE

Although it may seem like overkill, if you want to embellish the already extravagant Hollandaise Sauce, turn it into Béarnaise with the addition of shallots and tarragon, white wine, and white wine vinegar. Delicious! We particularly like it with swordfish, and of course it's a natural with filet mignon and prime rib.

MAKES ABOUT 2 CUPS

  1 tablespoon white wine vinegar
  1 tablespoon dry white wine
  1 teaspoon dried tarragon
  ½ teaspoon chopped shallots
  2 cups Hollandaise Sauce (page 212)
  Salt

1. In a small saucepan over medium heat, combine the vinegar, wine, tarragon, and shallots. Cook for 2 to 3 minutes, or until enough liquid evaporates so that it barely coats the bottom of the pan.

2. In the top of a double boiler set over simmering water, heat the Hollandaise Sauce, whisking to keep it from separating. Add the vinegar-shallot mixture and continue whisking. Season to taste with a little salt.

CREAM SAUCE

Our Cream Sauce is a thin roux, a flour-based sauce enriched with butter and smoothed with milk and cream. It's a versatile sauce for any number of dishes, such as casseroles and pasta sauces as well as the Broiled Lemon Chicken with Linguini (page 151).

MAKES ABOUT 5 CUPS

¼ cup plus 1 tablespoon **Clarified Butter** (page 231)
¼ cup **all-purpose flour**
4 cups **whole milk**
2 tablespoons **minced Spanish onion**
1¾ cups **heavy cream**
1¾ teaspoons **salt**
¾ teaspoon **freshly ground white pepper**

1. In a medium saucepan over low heat, heat the butter until hot. Whisk in the flour until smooth, and cook the roux gently for 8 minutes.

2. Meanwhile, in another medium saucepan, bring the milk to a boil over medium-high heat. Add to the roux with the onion and whisk well. Bring to a simmer, reduce the heat to low, and simmer, stirring frequently, for about 30 minutes, or until thickened.

3. In a small pan, heat the cream over medium-high heat just until it begins to steam. Pour into the sauce, add the salt and pepper, and mix well.

4. Strain the sauce through a chinois or a fine-mesh sieve into a metal bowl. Use immediately or put the bowl in a larger bowl filled with ice and water and let cool. When cool, cover with plastic wrap and refrigerate for up to 24 hours. Reheat over low heat until hot.

BEURRE BLANC

This is a standard cream sauce used in a number of our recipes. It's a French-style sauce (if anyone knows great sauces, it's the French!), easy to make and endlessly versatile. Cooking the wine until it nearly evaporates adds great flavor to the sauce, and adding the butter a tablespoon at a time turns it silken. Take your time when you make this; you will be rewarded with a smooth, satiny sauce with subtle but gorgeous flavor. We serve it with salmon, and of course it's integral to Chicken Christopher (page 146) and Shrimp Alexander (page 156).

MAKES ABOUT 2 CUPS

1 teaspoon Clarified Butter (page 231) **or olive oil**
1 large shallot, minced (about ¼ cup)
⅓ cup dry white wine
¾ cup heavy cream
¾ cup (1½ sticks) **unsalted butter, softened**
1 teaspoon fresh lemon juice
¼ teaspoon salt
Freshly ground white pepper

1. In a medium saucepan, heat the Clarified Butter over medium-low heat. Add the shallot and sauté for 2 to 3 minutes, or until it softens without coloring. Add the wine, raise the heat to medium-high, and bring to a boil. Reduce the heat and simmer for 3 to 4 minutes, or until the wine reduces and the liquid coats the bottom of the pan. Add the cream and simmer, stirring often, for 5 to 7 minutes, or until reduced by half.

2. Reduce the heat to low and begin adding the butter, a tablespoon at a time, whisking after each addition. Do not allow the cream to boil once the butter is added.

3. Remove the pan from the heat. Using a handheld immersion blender, beat for 5 to 10 seconds, or until smooth. Lift the beater and then immerse again and beat for a few seconds. Repeat this process to produce a silken sauce. If you do not have a handheld immersion blender, do this in an electric mixer or by hand. The immersion blender does the best job.

4. Add the lemon juice and salt and season to taste with pepper. Stir to blend. Strain the sauce through a fine-mesh sieve or a chinois into a small saucepan.

5. Keep the sauce warm over low heat, making sure the temperature remains 110° to 120°F. for up to 1 hour, or until ready to serve.

CELEBRITY CLIP

When stand-up comedian and television star George Lopez celebrated his birthday at Arnie Morton's in Los Angeles, he indulged in our shrimp cocktail and a filet mignon. Joining him at the table were actors Andy Garcia and Cheech Marin, and Kiss guitarist Paul Stanley. We surprised Lopez with three birthday cakes!

WHIPPED HORSERADISH

This is a simple sauce that looks and tastes more complicated than it is. When we first opened Morton's, we served freshly grated horseradish with our steaks and prime rib, but our guests complained it was too hot. We turned to a commercial bottled product (we like the creamy commercial brands more than the more briny ones), added heavy cream and mustard, and came up with this truly great sauce. It's good with beef—I really like it with the Cajun Ribeye Steak (page 104)—and even smoked salmon.

MAKES ABOUT 3½ CUPS

1 cup prepared horseradish
2 cups heavy cream
1 teaspoon Dijon mustard
¾ teaspoon salt
¾ teaspoon freshly ground white pepper
¾ teaspoon Tabasco sauce

1. Line a fine-mesh sieve with cheesecloth. Strain the horseradish for 2 to 3 minutes, or until reduced to ¾ cup. Press on the horseradish with a spoon or squeeze the cheesecloth to extract all the liquid.

2. In a mixing bowl, whip the cream with a wire whisk until it thickens to the consistency of sour cream. You can do this in an electric mixer set on medium-high speed, but watch carefully so that the cream does not overwhip.

3. Add the horseradish, mustard, salt, pepper, and Tabasco sauce. Whisk until thickened using a wire whisk or electric mixer. The sauce should be moist and the consistency of whipped cream.

4. Refrigerate for at least 1 hour, then serve immediately or transfer to a covered storage container and refrigerate for up to 1 day.

APRICOT CHUTNEY

When you read through the ingredients for this sauce, you might wonder how this could be anything special. Try it! It has sweetness, saltiness, and heat, and tastes great with scallops, pork, and lamb, and on steak sandwiches. It would even taste good on a tuna sandwich. Our senior vice president of operations, Kevin Weinert, came up with this years ago, and it's been so successful at Morton's that we've never looked back!

MAKES ABOUT 3 CUPS

1 tablespoon plus 1 teaspoon whole black peppercorns
2 cups prepared horseradish (16 ounces)
2 cups apricot preserves (one 18-ounce jar or a little more)

1. Put the peppercorns on a cutting board. Crush them by pressing down on them with the bottom of a heavy saucepan.

2. In a fine-mesh sieve or another sieve lined with cheesecloth, strain the horseradish for 2 to 3 minutes, or until reduced to 1 tightly packed cup. Press on the horseradish with a spoon or squeeze the cheesecloth to extract all the liquid.

3. In a small bowl, whisk the apricot preserves until smooth. Whisk in the strained horseradish and crushed peppercorns.

4. Serve immediately or transfer to a covered storage container and refrigerate for up to 3 days.

DIABLO SAUCE

We serve this with our Beef Tenderloin Brochettes (page 134), but you could serve it with chicken or pork. Keep a jar in the refrigerator for up to a week, particularly in the summer when you are grilling often. This is an instance where a handheld immersion blender works better than any other kitchen appliance.

MAKES ABOUT 2½ CUPS

1 tablespoon flavorless vegetable oil,
   such as canola or safflower
1¼ cups chopped Spanish onion (1 large onion)
2 tablespoons freshly cracked black peppercorns
½ cup plus 1 tablespoon dry white wine
½ cup plus 1 tablespoon distilled white vinegar
1 cup store-bought veal demi-glace (see Note, page 111)
1 cup heavy cream
¼ teaspoon Tabasco sauce
1 tablespoon unsalted butter
2 tablespoons plus 1½ teaspoons all-purpose flour
½ to ¾ teaspoon Kitchen Bouquet (see Note)
¼ teaspoon salt
⅛ teaspoon freshly ground white pepper

1. In a medium saucepan, heat the oil over medium heat. Add the onion and sauté with the peppercorns for 4 to 6 minutes, stirring often, or until the onion is lightly browned.

2. Add the white wine and vinegar, raise the heat to medium-high, and simmer for 3 to 4 minutes, or until the liquid is reduced by a third. (This would be about ⅔ cup liquid.) Add the demi-glace and then slowly pour in the cream. Bring the liquid to a boil over medium-high heat. Reduce the heat to medium and stir in the Tabasco sauce.

3. Remove the pan from the heat. Using a handheld immersion blender, blend for 1 minute, or until the onion is puréed and the sauce is smooth. (Alternatively, purée the sauce in a blender. You will have to do this in batches.)

4. Meanwhile, in a small pan, melt the butter over medium heat. Add the flour, a few teaspoons at a time, and whisk to blend. When all the flour is added, the roux will be thick and smooth. Stir into the sauce and cook over medium heat for 3 to 5 minutes, stirring constantly, or until the sauce has thickened. Stir in the Kitchen Bouquet and the salt and pepper. Taste and adjust the seasoning, if needed. Strain through a chinois or a fine-mesh sieve into a metal bowl. Submerge the bowl in a larger bowl filled with ice cubes and water and let the sauce cool. Cover and refrigerate until cold.

5. If using right away, reheat the sauce in a saucepan over medium heat until hot. Do not boil. If not, transfer to a tightly lidded container and refrigerate for up to 1 week.

Note: Kitchen Bouquet, sold in 4-ounce bottles in every supermarket, is used to brown and season gravies, stews, and other meat dishes.

MUSTARD-MAYONNAISE SAUCE

Mixing a little mustard into mayonnaise and giving it a little zing with Worcestershire sauce and horseradish translates into one of our most beloved sauces. Nothing could be easier. We serve this with our crab cakes and crabmeat canapés, as well as with our little steak sandwiches. You'll find many uses for this when you make sandwiches or serve seafood.

MAKES ABOUT 1¾ CUPS

$1^1/_2$ **cups mayonnaise**

3 tablespoons Dijon mustard

¾ teaspoon Worcestershire sauce

$1^1/_2$ **teaspoons prepared horseradish**

1. In a mixing bowl, stir together the mayonnaise, mustard, Worcestershire sauce, and horseradish. Whisk with a wire whisk until lightened and smooth.

2. Use immediately or transfer to a lidded container and refrigerate for up to 5 days.

GARLIC BUTTER

Our garlic butter is a little more involved than some, but it's absolutely sublime. It's so nicely seasoned that you can add it to plain vegetables, potatoes, pasta, or rice and not have any need for another seasoning. We love it with mushrooms. Try it with our mashed potatoes, and presto! Garlic mashed potatoes. You can make a lot at once—you could easily double this recipe—and keep it in the freezer for a month or two. Knowing it's right there makes home cooking so much easier. Don't be put off by the anchovies; they simply provide a depth of saltiness you can't get any other way.

MAKES ABOUT 2½ CUPS

2 tablespoons plus 1 teaspoon chopped garlic
2 tablespoons chopped peeled shallots
½ tablespoon rinsed, drained, and chopped anchovies (3 to 4 fillets)
½ bunch curly-leaf parsley, stems removed and discarded, chopped (about 1 cup)
1¾ cups (3½ sticks) **unsalted butter, softened**
½ tablespoon Pernod liqueur
2 teaspoons coarse salt
1 teaspoon freshly ground white pepper

1. In the bowl of a food processor fitted with a metal blade, pulse the garlic, shallots, anchovies, and parsley until finely chopped.

2. In the bowl of an electric mixer fitted with the paddle attachment and set on medium speed, beat the butter for 1 minute. Scrape the garlic mixture into the butter and beat for another minute or so until thoroughly mixed. Reduce the speed to low. Add the Pernod, salt, and pepper and beat to mix. Increase the speed to high and mix for 2 minutes, or until the butter is smooth, fluffy, and light. Scrape down the sides of the bowl with a rubber spatula. Mix the butter mixture for 2 more minutes at high speed.

3. Use immediately or transfer to an airtight container. Refrigerate for up to 5 days, or wrap well and freeze for up to 2 months.

COCKTAIL SAUCE

Thick and bold, never wimpy, this cocktail sauce is the perfect complement to our jumbo shrimp. Without a doubt, you will find many other uses for it, from serving alongside grilled shrimp to accenting a crabmeat cocktail.

MAKES ABOUT 2 CUPS

1/2 **cup prepared horseradish**
1¾ **cups bottled chili sauce** (one 12-ounce bottle)
¾ **teaspoon Worcestershire sauce**
¾ **teaspoon fresh lemon juice**
Salt and freshly ground white pepper

1. Line a fine-mesh sieve with cheesecloth. Strain the horseradish in the sieve for 2 to 3 minutes, or until reduced to ¼ cup. Squeeze the cheesecloth to extract all the liquid.

2. In a small mixing bowl, combine the strained horseradish, chili sauce, Worcestershire sauce, and lemon juice. Season to taste with salt and pepper. Whisk until completely blended.

3. Serve immediately or transfer to a covered storage container and refrigerate for 5 to 7 days. For the best flavor, let the sauce sit in the refrigerator for at least 1 day.

CLASSIC VINAIGRETTE

Most good home cooks have a favorite vinaigrette. This is ours. If you haven't perfected yours yet, this may become the dressing you make time and again for green salads, tomato salads, and grilled vegetable salads. Make this well ahead of time and let it sit at room temperature so that the flavors can blend.

MAKES ABOUT 2½ CUPS

1 cup flavorless vegetable oil,
    such as canola or safflower
½ cup white wine vinegar
2 tablespoons balsamic vinegar
½ cup finely minced red bell pepper
⅓ cup finely minced white onion
1½ teaspoons finely minced garlic
1½ teaspoons salt
½ teaspoon freshly ground white pepper

1. In a medium bowl, whisk together the oil and vinegars. Add the red pepper, onion, garlic, salt, and pepper and whisk until well mixed.

2. Transfer to a lidded glass or rigid plastic container and allow to sit at room temperature for 12 hours before using. The vinaigrette will keep for up to 1 week in the refrigerator. Allow to reach room temperature and shake well before using.

DIJON VINAIGRETTE

Our chefs used to spend hours chopping red bell peppers, onions, and garlic, as well as other ingredients, to make a full-bodied, mustard-based vinaigrette, which we served with our Chopped Salad (page 78). One day, chef Chris Rook was making this at home and, to save time, tossed in a packet of Good Seasons salad dressing mix. Much to his surprise, the result was just as good as our labor-intensive original! Try this with any green salad.

MAKES ABOUT 2½ CUPS

$\frac{2}{3}$ **cup white balsamic vinegar**
$\frac{1}{2}$ **cup Dijon mustard**
**3½ tablespoons Italian salad dressing mix,
   such as Good Seasons** (see Note)
1 cup extra-virgin olive oil

1. In a medium mixing bowl, combine the vinegar and $\frac{1}{3}$ cup of water. Whisk in the mustard and salad dressing mix until well mixed. Add the olive oil and whisk until the dressing is emulsified.

2. Let the dressing rest for a few minutes before using so that the flavors can blend. Refrigerate in a tightly lidded glass or rigid plastic container for up to 7 days and whisk before using.

Note: If you use Good Seasons brand mix, two packets work well.

MORTON'S BLUE CHEESE DRESSING

Our blue cheese dressing is legendary. The original recipe came from Arnie Morton's mother, who created it for the restaurant she and her husband owned when Arnie was growing up. When Arnie and I opened Morton's Steakhouse in 1978, we put the dressing on our menu. Although we had the recipe, it just wasn't quite right. Arnie sought out the pantry cook who had originally made it for his parents. Miss May, as she was called, was quite elderly by then. But she came in and taught us how to achieve the right consistency. The trick? Miss May used her hands to mix the dressing ever so gently so that it remained chunky. Like us, you might prefer a rubber spatula, but use a light hand. This is the dressing to serve with Morton's Salad (page 84), and it would be equally delicious with just about any other green salad, sliced tomatoes, or served as a dip.

MAKES ABOUT 3 CUPS

2 cups mayonnaise (see Note)
1 cup plus 2 tablespoons sour cream
¼ cup buttermilk
1 teaspoon Durkee Famous Sauce (see Note)
½ teaspoon seasoned salt
Salt and freshly ground black pepper
7 ounces blue cheese, crumbled (about 1½ cups)

1. In a large mixing bowl, whisk together the mayonnaise and sour cream. Add the buttermilk, Durkee sauce, and seasoned salt. Whisk until well mixed. Season to taste with salt and pepper and whisk again.

2. Using a rubber spatula, gently fold in the blue cheese. Transfer to a storage container with a tight-fitting lid and refrigerate for at least 1 day and up to 4 days.

Notes: Use real mayonnaise, such as Kraft or Best Foods (Hellmann's), and not a related product such as Miracle Whip or light mayonnaise. At Morton's we use Kraft Real Mayonnaise. When writing this book, we tried making the dressing with Miracle Whip, and the finished product turned thin and milky when it was stored for more than a day.

Durkee Famous Sauce is sold in many supermarkets. It's a vinegar-flavored, mustard-mayonnaise type of sauce. If you cannot locate it, use our recipe for Mustard-Mayonnaise Sauce on page 222.

CAESAR DRESSING

Everyone loves Caesar salad, and the dressing makes or breaks it. This one is a winner. We no longer make our dressing tableside, as we did when we first opened. But we have not skimped on the real ingredients we use in the dressing. You make this in a food processor, so it's extremely simple. It keeps in the refrigerator for 3 or 4 days.

MAKES ABOUT 3½ CUPS

3 large eggs
Two 2-ounce cans anchovies packed in oil,
    rinsed, patted dry, and diced
1½ tablespoons Dijon mustard
1 tablespoon garlic powder
2 teaspoons anchovy paste
1 teaspoon freshly ground white pepper
1½ cups flavorless vegetable oil, such as
    canola or safflower
⅓ cup red wine vinegar
2 tablespoons fresh lemon juice
½ cup finely grated Parmesan cheese

1. In the bowl of a food processor fitted with a metal blade, combine the eggs, anchovies, mustard, garlic powder, anchovy paste, and pepper. Process for about 2 minutes, or until thoroughly mixed.

2. With the motor running, slowly add the oil until emulsified and the consistency of thin mayonnaise. Add the vinegar and lemon juice. Mix until the dressing is well combined. With the motor still running, add the Parmesan. Scrape down the sides of the bowl and then mix the dressing for 30 seconds.

3. Refrigerate the dressing for at least 1 hour, or until chilled. Use the dressing immediately or transfer to a covered storage container and refrigerate for up to 4 days.

CLARIFIED BUTTER

Once you get into the habit of clarifying butter, you will find it is not much of a hassle. Clarified butter can be heated to higher temperatures, and because the milk solids have been removed, it keeps very well. When refrigerated, it solidifies and turns a little grainy, but it melts easily and becomes liquid again. We use it throughout the book because it does not burn easily.

MAKES 1 CUP

15 tablespoons unsalted butter
9 tablespoons unsalted margarine

1. In a small saucepan over medium heat, combine the butter and margarine. Cook for about 5 minutes, or until completely melted and simmering gently.

2. Remove from the heat and let stand at room temperature for about 10 minutes, or until the solids settle on the bottom of the pan. Skim the foam off the top and discard.

3. Carefully pour or ladle the clear, liquid butter into a storage container and leave the milk solids in the pan. Discard the solids. Let the butter cool and then refrigerate the clarified butter for up to 1 week.

ALEX'S BREAD CRUMBS

I can't emphasize enough how easy it is to make your own bread crumbs and how much better they taste than those dried-out crumbs you buy at the supermarket. It's a snap to make fresh bread into crumbs in the food processor or blender. And while this recipe doesn't call for stale bread, if you let the bread sit on the counter-top for an hour or two, it will make great crumbs. I suggest you pat the garlic and shallot dry before adding them to the crumbs for more efficient mixing. We use these to bread shrimp, cod, and chicken—you'll use them for all sorts of recipes that call for bread crumbs.

MAKES ABOUT 2 CUPS

8 ounces firm white bread (4 to 5 slices)
5 teaspoons minced garlic
2 teaspoons minced shallot
2 teaspoons chopped fresh curly-leaf parsley
Salt and freshly ground white pepper

1. Slice the crusts from the bread and then cut the bread into large chunks. Discard the crusts or reserve them for another use.

2. In the bowl of a food processor fitted with a metal blade, grind the bread to fine crumbs. Transfer the crumbs to a mixing bowl.

3. Pat the garlic and shallot dry with a paper towel. Add to the bread crumbs and toss to mix. Add the parsley, toss, and season to taste with salt and pepper. Mix well. Use right away or store the bread crumbs in a tightly covered container for up to 24 hours.

Klaus Fritsch, second from right, in 1985 at the opening of the first Morton's in Denver. He is surrounded by Arnie Morton's family. From left: Arnie's wife, Zorine; Arnie; his son David; and Arnie's daughter, Amy.

ACKNOWLEDGMENTS

A book about a restaurant such as Morton's Steak-house owes a debt to many people, all of whom have contributed to making us as good as we are today.

First, I want to thank Arnie Morton, who died in the spring of 2005 and who, for many years, was my trusted partner and friend. Arnie's vision for the restaurants was brilliant, and he never wavered from his original idea of a top-quality steakhouse that would, in his words, be a neighborhood saloon for the rich!

Thanks, too, to Morton's Restaurant Group chairman emeritus Allen J. Bernstein; chairman, CEO, and president Thomas J. Baldwin; and to Morton's Steakhouse former president John Bettin, all of whom supported this book wholeheartedly. And thanks to Kevin Weinert, senior vice president of operations, who helped with some of the recipes and all of the reminiscences. Without Raki Mehra's steeltrap memory, some of the old stories might have been forgotten. Raki is the general manager and maître d' at our original State Street restaurant, has been with us forever, and pretty much knows all there is to know about the workings of the restaurant. Thanks to Roger Drake, vice president of communications for Morton's Restaurant Group, who saw this project through from idea to final book.

Thanks to Chris Rook, our corporate chef, who made sure the recipes were accurate and on target for the home cook, and who was always available for questions and problem-solving. Thanks to Tylor Field III, vice president of wine and spirits, for help with the cocktail recipes. Thanks to Peggy Reilly, who coordinated the delivery of meat to our recipe tester and who supplied our writer with hard-to-find recipes and essential information.

Thanks especially to Mary Goodbody, who worked with Chris, Roger, and me to get our recipes and philosophy onto the pages of a book. Thanks to Deborah Callan, who tested all the recipes so that they work so beautifully in home kitchens. Thanks to Lisa Thornton, Francine Fielding, and Rachel Deming. A special thanks to our Stamford, Connecticut Morton's, which as the restaurant nearest to Mary and Deborah helped them in several ways. Our Stamford staff personally delivered a cooler of meat to Mary early one rainy morning in a parking lot in Fairfield, Connecticut.

A special thank you to our vendor partners Brown-Forman Beverages and Ste. Michelle Wine Estates for their involvement in the cookbook tour.

A big thanks to Jane Dystel, our literary agent, who helped us find Mary and then find a publisher. A huge thanks to everyone at Clarkson Potter, including our first editor, Chris Pavone, and his assistant, Adina Steiman. Thanks to Rica Allannic, who stepped in during the final days of editing and saw the book through to print. Rica worked with Chris, Roger, and me when we traveled to New York for the photo shoot. A warm thanks to David Prince and his team for the amazing photographs.

Finally, a heartfelt thanks to our guests, who with their loyalty and enthusiasm have made Morton's Steakhouses from New York to San Francisco to Singapore the phenomenal success they are.

INDEX

Note: Page numbers in **bold** refer to photographs.

CONVERSION CHART
EQUIVALENT IMPERIAL AND METRIC MEASUREMENTS

American cooks use standard containers, the 8-ounce cup and a tablespoon that takes exactly 16 level fillings to fill that cup level. Measuring by cup makes it very difficult to give weight equivalents, as a cup of densely packed butter will weigh considerably more than a cup of flour. The easiest way therefore to deal with cup measurements in recipes is to take the amount by volume rather than by weight. Thus the equation reads:

1 cup = 240 ml = 8 fl. oz.   ½ cup = 120 ml = 4 fl. oz.

In the States, butter is often measured in sticks. One stick is the equivalent of 8 tablespoons. One tablespoon of butter is therefore equivalent to ½ ounce/15 grams.

LIQUID MEASURES

Fluid Ounces	U.S.	Imperial	Milliliters
⅛	1 teaspoon	1 teaspoon	5
¼	2 teaspoons	1 dessertspoon	10
½	1 tablespoon	1 tablespoon	14
1	2 tablespoons	2 tablespoons	28
2	¼ cup	4 tablespoons	56
4	½ cup		120
5		¼ pint or 1 gill	140
6	¾ cup		170
8	1 cup		240
9			250, ¼ liter
10	1¼ cups	½ pint	280
12	1½ cups		340
15		¾ pint	420
16	2 cups		450
18	2¼ cups		500, ½ liter
20	2½ cups	1 pint	560
24	3 cups		675
25		1¼ pints	700
27	3½ cups		750
30	3¾ cups	1½ pints	840
32	4 cups or 1 quart		900
35		1¾ pints	980
36	4½ cups		1000, 1 liter
40	5 cups	2 pints or 1 quart	1120

SOLID MEASURES

U.S. AND IMPERIAL MEASURES		METRIC MEASURES	
Ounces	Pounds	Grams	Kilos
1		28	
2		56	
3½		100	
4	¼	112	
5		140	
6		168	
8	½	225	
9		250	¼
12	¾	340	
16	1	450	
18		500	½
20	1¼	560	
24	1½	675	
27		750	¾
28	1¾	780	
32	2	900	
36	2¼	1000	1
40	2½	1100	
48	3	1350	
54		1500	1½

OVEN TEMPERATURE EQUIVALENTS

Fahrenheit	Celsius	Gas Mark	Description
225	110	¼	Cool
250	130	½	
275	140	1	Very Slow
300	150	2	
325	170	3	Slow
350	180	4	Moderate
375	190	5	
400	200	6	Moderately Hot
425	220	7	Fairly Hot
450	230	8	Hot
475	240	9	Very Hot
500	250	10	Extremely Hot

Any broiling recipes can be used with the grill of the oven, but beware of high-temperature grills.

EQUIVALENTS FOR INGREDIENTS

all-purpose flour—plain flour
baking sheet—oven tray
buttermilk—ordinary milk
cheesecloth—muslin
coarse salt—kitchen salt
cornstarch—cornflour
eggplant—aubergine

granulated sugar—castor sugar
half and half—12% fat milk
heavy cream—double cream
light cream—single cream
lima beans—broad beans
parchment paper—greaseproof paper
plastic wrap—cling film

scallion—spring onion
shortening—white fat
unbleached flour—strong, white flour
vanilla bean—vanilla pod
zest—rind
zucchini—courgettes or marrow